THIS NEW SEASON

Our class, our schools, our world.

Chris Searle

Give me a reason
This new season
Who I saw
I see no more

When I looked round
There on the ground

I found the question, Why
And I saw a little boy cry

Charlie Mason, 12

Calder & Boyars
London

First published in Great Britain in 1973
by Calder and Boyars Ltd.
18 Brewer Street, London W1

ISBN 0 7145 0972 8 Casebound Edition
ISBN 0 7145 1047 5 Paper Edition

All royalties from this book will go to help support a Community
Law Centre in Stepney.

Printed in Great Britain by
Biddles Ltd., Guildford, Surrey

CONTENTS

To
My Mother and Father
and
Rob, Ron, Linda and all Stepney children
like Nancy,
and all those friends
who stood up for me
and *Stepney Words*.

PREFACE

'. . . intellectual alienation is a creation of middle class society. What I call middle class society is any society that becomes rigidified in predetermined forms, forbidding all evolution, all gains, all progress, all discovery. I call middle class a closed society in which life has no taste, in which the air is tainted, in which ideas and men are corrupt. And I think that a man who takes a stand against this death is in a sense a revolutionary.'

FRANTZ FANON*

Ruling class State power translates and mediates itself to its subjects through its servant institutions. One of its major tools is the School, the bastion of its servant culture, the white middle class consciousness. The teacher becomes the functionary of State power, imbuing the children with State-licensed knowledge and ideology.

Many times in these pages I use the words 'white middle class consciousness'. Within this concept is a power which has spread itself so mercilessly through our culture and political system that its definitions and structure have become almost lost to us. The received and accepted surburban morality of isolated individuality and competition, where minds grow apart and divided from each other, where it is seen as weak and characterless to depend on collective strength and identity, and where the self becomes a motor on his own road, is the morality being inculcated into our children by middle class family life and schooling. It is a morality which serves the profit maker and denies and betrays democratic advancement.

* Black Skins, White Masks, p. 160 *(Paladin Books)*

It is the morality of exploitation, capital, and the economic and social domination of one man over another. It represents the standards that benefit and perpetuate the status-quo, the money-loving and the hierarchical. It is the culture of men who disbelieve in each other, who are alienated and cynical and flounder in absurdity and despair. It is the anti-culture of men who have no faith in working together and deciding together. It is the way of life we have to challenge and overcome if we are to create equity and equality in our society, and thus in our schools. As teachers and workers, we can only break this consciousness by driving it from ourselves, and working to destroy it in our lives and schools as rank and file trade unionists who are working and thinking collectively. Teachers are the group most easily sucked towards the middle class syndrome, and who become the most powerful agents for spreading the received and established anti-culture.

What so many teachers are afraid of is a recognition of their own exploited position, in educating working class children merely to the level of objects to be manipulated by the interests of a profit motivated, anti-human culture. This recognition would then be followed by changing sides, changing class allegiances, moving from being confused liberals, worriedly but guiltily caulking up the cracks and contradictions in the status-quo, to serious socialists, out to undermine and destroy it, replacing it with an alternative that serves all children, excites all generous spirits, and fulfils all human potentialities. A teacher, as one who promotes and develops human rationality, generosity and equity, can give no real and positive social love to the children he teaches, without an analysis of the social reality within which they all live and connect. And without belonging to the working class people he teaches and sharing their energies and causes, his assumed loyalty to their development will only ever be nominal, and very often negative, as he will be promoting a culture inimical to the working class interest, a culture of exploitation and betrayal.

Now we must re-establish culture in its organic, democratic sense, linking it to the real world of people who are working and struggling for control over the conditions of their lives. As teachers, it is only by completely committing ourselves to their struggles that we can commit ourselves to a truly educational consciousness. The 'Problem of Education' cannot be isolated merely as a problem of schools, or of teachers. It is a problem of politics, and the economic domination of one class over another. It has to be solved politically, in the schools as in all of society. We cannot afford to divert ourselves with notions of de-schooling when we need more schools, more teachers, more books, more facilities for our working class children, more concentration to develop their frustrated and insulted potential. The more economic and educational demands we make for our class, the working class, the more we threaten the prevailing standards peddled in the schools which divide us from ourselves and each other and weaken our strength with their mystification. We have to confront the enormity of the problem as an organised and inter-related body: teachers, parents, and school students. We can educate for stoicism and acceptance, only passing onto our children the identity of the exploited and underdeveloped, or we can educate for struggle and solidarity, showing our children that we are fighting and learning with them, affirming ourselves, our class, and our right and determination to control our own social and educational future.

DIVIDE AND SCHOOL

My teacher's like a battle tank
Roaring at the enemy
The enemy is us
And the roaring is the lessons.
He keeps us in a prison camp
Torturing us each day
And he will keep on torturing us
Till our minds are worn away.

Roderick, 13.

*The only way the exploiter can maintain his
position is to create differences and maintain
deformities.*

George Jackson. *

Because we live in a capitalist society, we live in a society which
creates and thrives on divisions. People are divided from themselves
and each other on every level of life. 'Divide and school' is only one
level: the working class child and the teacher, two of the most
exploited sections of the community, are made to fight it out in the
classroom. The classroom becomes an arena where teacher and child
are forced by a common enemy to contest against each other. The
teacher is seen by his superiors in the hierarchical structure within
which he operates as their servant. He sells his labour to the State and
signs a contract which confirms this, a contract binding him in a
servant/master relationship with his employers. He does not sign a

* Blood in my Eye, p. 204, *(Cape, 1972)*

contract of service to those children and parents with whom he is going to work. He is not at school to serve the local community, he is contracted as the agent of repression in a social machine out to exploit and mould children to suit the ends of a brutal system which serves the profit makers. The child is seen statistically, as mere raw material to fill up the functions for making profit. The teacher is delegated the squalid job of persuading or coercing the child to cross the line — to sit quietly and contentedly at a job which will give him no chance to participate in the government of his own life, no opportunity to make the decisions affecting the conditions of his life, only to produce, consume and live 'normally' like an automaton. If he is educated at all, he is educated for leisure, not for democratic power or the collective struggle for social equality.

There is no dignity in the teacher's job, no respect, unless he is struggling against this situation. How much respect for himself can a teacher have if he is educating children merely to accommodate them into slots provided by an exploiting society? Education and respect can only come together if Education is seen in terms of giving people the inspiration and confidence to take and control what is theirs, but what has been stolen from them. The idea that teachers can succeed educationally by merely being kind, accommodating or understanding in the accepted 'liberal' sense, is only to mystify the situation. It is a lie to pretend that British schools are fair, equitable places — they are hierarchical and undemocratic. Whether the true situation is concealed by liberalism or not, the social reality soon reveals itself to the child: there are the same class antagonisms, the same conditions of service to employers, the same dole queues, the same exploitation and hierarchical ladder, and the same disrespect for those who do not succeed in climbing up the rungs. The false smile can be worse than the cane. At least with the cane, the enemy is recognisable:

Why Keep the Cane?
from the Warden of Millfield School

Your correspondent Mary Ayres declares the cane to be 'a symbol of defeat.' It is surely no such thing, but is a symbol of power — the power which the young have to learn as soon as possible lies behind the law.

Children naturally tend to press the barriers encircling them, and probe for the weak spots through which to infiltrate as and when opportunity occurs. If authority is not equipped cap-a-pie to resist these pressures, then it will be overthrown, greatly to the disadvantage of all concerned — including the children.

Moral strength is not sufficient to cope with every situation arising in school life, and I believe that it is necessary that the young should be made to realise not only that behind the word of reproof is something hard that hurts, but that behind that something are the police and the armed services.

R.J.O MEYER, Street, Somerset.
(A letter published in the 'Daily Telegraph'
19.12.'71)

The classroom is the centre of the most political conflict. The teacher, the force acting on the established culture's behalf, is there to break the working class child's confidence in his own individual and collective identity, and make him easier to manipulate and manage by his future employers. The child's rebellion is smashed because it is the most dangerous of rebellions. If the child knows that he can successfully challenge the teacher, he will think that he can challenge his masters on every subsequent situation in life. And the teacher — underpaid, confused, frightened, trying to square his own situation with his honesty — is the steward of an offensive consciousness who is paid by his employers to put down or divert any sign of the energy of that rebellion. Like other workers, the teacher is on the point of production, but his product is teenaged human units. The teacher and child are forced onto the opposite sides of the battle-line continuously by the same enemy. The teacher of working class children is often trapped in the same situation as the British soldier in Belfast or Londonderry. He finds himself fighting people who are really on his side because they both have a common enemy. And that enemy has divided them and is exploiting them both. Only by embracing their apparent, imposed enemies across the battle-line and turning together to fight the real enemy who has set them against each other, can they ever move to have more control over their lives.

The child may recognise that the traditional educational roles have polarised into a state of enmity, and that unless he protects himself, he will always be the loser:

13

Too much class work
Too much home work
Laugh at his jokes
Not at your own
I do not like him
He does not like me
We are both even
Except he has a belt
That is my teacher

Billy, 14.

The teacher has to obey the procedures of the schools and train
the children for the examination system. It very often frustrates him,
and it frustrates the children, who may be looking for an education
far broader and more meaningful. The child and teacher are not
allowed to educate each other, they must keep inside the narrow
gauge of the syllabus created by others who are called superiors. If
they break, they are both labelled failures, misfits. They recognise
each other's absurdity, but feel helpless and cynical. They begin to
shout at each other and hate each other. The success of 'divide and
school' appears complete:

SCHOOL

The middle of the longest term of the year
All work, all work.
The teachers have started to get fed up.
The screams and shouts are getting too much.
And I sit here staring into space
Not listening to a word that's said.

The middle of term, so work must be done,
For the exams that come near the end.
Everything we have learned is being learned to us again,
And I sit here staring into space
While the day goes by and by.

14

The teachers are getting restless now.
Why will the children not learn?
They just sit here and scream and shout,
They think it's a waste of time,
But it's the profession they choose
So shouting and screaming must be suffered.
So they must keep on
They must keep on speaking their knowledge all day.
Because the pupils must be learned
For the exam that comes at the end of the year.

Lorraine, 15.

The teacher is contracted to be the steward of the white middle class consciousness. He is instructed to heave the accepted, respectable white middle class mind onto the child whatever the child's background or particular community. 'Get on with your work,' says the teacher to the child, when really it is the syllabus of the established middle class culture promoted by the teacher that he wants the child to get on with, not the child's own. The child is not allowed to discover his own life and identity, only the life which the teacher keeps for him. The working class child must forget his own community, his own people, his own loyalties, and make new ones. He is forced to change identities. His old identity is gradually and calculatedly broken. He must not allow his working class reality to enter the classroom. In 1971, in Croydon, England, a 13-year old boy whose mother was a lavatory cleaner, was suspended from his school by the Headmaster for writing about his own 'Family Life'. The Headmaster said this essay was 'obscene and derisory'.

FAMILY LIFE

'In my house everybody is happy but sometimes there are arguments. The house we live in has three bedrooms two toilets a kitchen, a dining room, a living room and a bathroom. We live at Bridle Road, Shirley, Croydon.
My father has just built a porch on the front of our house this

is because in the winter the cold air comes under the door but now it won't.

I would like my house to be a big one and a modern one, maybe in the country. But as you see my hopes are very low and I would like two children a boy and a girl. When I am sixteen I am going to be a bank clerk and play football go fishing and find a girl freind. But as well here you can see that also is impossible.

If I get the money I will move to the continent and live in the jungle like tarzen. I will bring back animals to eat and kill lions and fight giant snakes. I will by crusiers and sail up the jungle rivers and soon I would come back and live in England with all my trophies of lions, elephants tigers buffolo and act. But also this is a dream a dream world just a dream world so as I have had my dreams I shall go back to work as a public lavatory cleaner.'

Martin, 13.

Instead, the child is told that he must adopt the teacher's attitudes and selection of facts, not his own. Ultimately, the selection of facts and attitudes for a child's education 'the curriculum' will be a political act, and the attitudes and facts given to the child by the teacher will be those chosen and approved by the social machine and 'superiors' whom the teacher serves. And for the working class child, the curriculum of the schools is a part of an alien culture, a culture that has always been his enemy and betrayer.

In any 'divide and school' situation the children are the colonised, the exploited. They are held down by the threats and weapons of the teachers serving the educational machine. So if the divisions between teachers and children begin to heal and the enmity begins to break down, the schools begin to lose their social function as training grounds for obedience to the established order. How will the people submit easily any more? How will they be so easily pushed around and manipulated to fit into the spaces of the world made for them by the powerful? Divide and school, divide the teachers from the children, and there you have in miniature the syndrome of society: those who rule, those who obey. Get the children to accept that at school, and they will accept it all their lives. They'll kick against each other, hate each other, contest with each other, just to gain the most favour with the teachers and get the best plums. The teacher is 'Sir' — it is the old, feudal master/servant relationship. The teacher is the officer class, the staff room is his mess. He expects obedience from his underlings and expects his officer colleagues to close ranks against the children in times of crisis as in pupils' strikes, or when he beats a child and perhaps goes 'a little too far'. He owes obedience himself to the generals well behind the lines on the governing body. As an eminent Vice-Chairman of Governors said at an educational meeting concerning children in school: 'When I was in the Army we always obeyed an order before we ever thought of questioning it.'

The teacher in the British state school finds himself in a totally divided situation. When he leaves college or university he joins a school and becomes a probationary teacher, stepping onto the lowest rung of the school hierarchical ladder. He is at the base of a scale of salary differentials which lures him upwards and onwards. If he behaves himself in his probationary year, he will find that promotion is open to him. The Headmaster is in complete control of the 'internal organisation, management and discipline of the school', as well as having the power to 'exercise supervision over the teaching and non-teaching staff' (1944 Education Act). If the teacher pleases the Head, he may allocate salary increases to him, in the form of scaled or graded posts, or the teacher may feel inclined to apply for other posts at other schools where there is a vacant and more highly-paid post. This situation causes huge instability in the schools: the teachers compete and scramble amongst each other for the Headmasters' favours and the special allowances, and the Head's own autocracy is confirmed and strengthened. He has a divided, competing staff who are more interested in manipulating each other than challenging his power: he continues to rule as he simultaneously divides any potential opposition. The classroom teacher* remains unrepresented: it is his task to teach, not to govern or form policy. Teachers, particularly young teachers, become nomadic in outlook, moving from school to school for improved allowances. The stability

---

* The classroom teacher who is with the children, teaching all day, is called an 'assistant teacher'. The non-teaching administrator who sits in his office all day is called the 'Head Teacher'. A schools' inspector of 30 years experience said recently: 'The job of the assistant teacher is to assist the Head.'

of the school and the pupils' relationships with the younger teachers are weakened. The pupils become cynical about trusting their teachers who always seem to be moving on, and the divisions widen. Ultimately, the only remedy for this situation is a single, unified salary scale which will both prevent the destructive mobility of teachers, and the squalid scramble for the extra allowances.

Mostly, teachers — particularly teachers in working class areas — do not live in the area where they teach. They are divided from the living experiences of the children whom they teach, and the children's parents. They become commuters, with a life at school, and a different life at home. Their attitudes become schizophrenic. They may have to reconcile work in an inner-city working class area with home in a more cosy, middle class suburb. They bring their home, suburban, attitudes to work with them, and they are immediately alienated from the people they teach. They are not neighbours to the children, they come from outside. When senior teachers or Headmasters earning £4-5,000 a year, living in prosperous garden suburbs in Essex commute to a decaying urban area like the East End of London to direct the educational strategies of an exploitative system, they are following the syndrome of the employer who manipulates his workers for his own profit from a secure, well-cushioned, outside situation. In Willmott's survey *Adolescent Boys of East London** a common enough complaint about their teachers from the boys was: 'They mostly lived quite a way out, at London Airport and Braintree and places like that.' The teachers were consequently seen as evangelists of a different kind of life with alien habits and experiences which they tried to inculcate into the boys, trying to substitute a new identity for the older, accepted one:

> 'The school was always trying to turn you into something you were not. The idea was to make you into a collar and tie type, and I didn't like that'.*

17-year old boy.

*(*Penguin, 1969*) p.89

The teacher is considered a 'professional man' and not a worker. 'Unprofessional conduct' is seen as one of the cardinal sins that a teacher should never commit. He is expected to maintain a level of 'professional disengagement' and formality with the children he teaches and their parents, to foster the atmosphere of good discipline. This has the expected divisive effect in a working class area:

> '. . . you see in this part of the world —
> it's not a professional part of the world, and
> a professional man doesn't really seem like
> one of us. You don't really accept him.'

18-year old boy.

To keep an authoritarian discipline, a teacher will fall back on his professional status, which finally, to himself, will give him indemnity from error. To working class children often mystified by the teacher's omniscient pose, that professional status may well be proof of the teacher's rectitude. His morality, along with his status, was always previously unquestioned. His class distinction also gave him an accepted moral superiority over the children he taught. Now, as the authoritarian notions of the teacher break down, children are simultaneously beginning to question everything about their teachers: detachment, aloofness, moral rectitude, and relevance of the teacher's knowledge and view of life. In such a situation, the idea of a teacher still retaining his 'professional disengagement' becomes an absurdity. He has to work much harder to prove his relevance and credibility. At last, the teacher will have to see himself not as a professional, but as another worker. He will have to climb right down from his artificial status:

> Teacher, teacher who are you,
> Sitting on your chair so tall,
> Tell me your name and what do you teach,
> Also pray tell me what do you eat?

Many people sit and stare

Not a problem — the educ. blnft has been called.

19

Watching your face with its frightening glare
Ranting and raving all day long
Not giving a thought to those who stare

Teacher, teacher who are you
Sitting on that chair so tall
Do you really cane, cook, eat and digest people?
If so, your mind is wanted elsewhere.

Sharon, 13.

For children born in Britain, education as a part of any social
opportunity is still a matter of chance:

THE CHANCE

Here I am lonely in my mother's womb
As I am lying here, I am wondering
Just whether to come out and see the bright world.
But maybe it is not a bright world,
It's maybe dull, but I can't tell
If it is a dull world,
I will not be able to get back into the womb if it is dull,
It is just a chance that I will have to take.

Timmy, 11.

The child has to take his chances in an inequitable and divided
society which gives little real credence to social equality. In England
there are fee-paying public schools, direct grant and grammar schools,
secondary modern schools, comprehensive schools, approved schools,
schools for those labelled 'educationally sub-normal' or 'maladjusted'.
There are now even special schools for truants. The divisions within
the educational system are only a symptom of divisions within the
social system. Most schools are still 'streamed'. Some large
comprehensives have as many as thirteen streams, and the children
know very clearly their placement in the divisions of their year. In

other schools the grading of the classes is concealed from the children and they have to guess where they are placed. In one school in outer London the grading is done by a secret password, with the sequence of the letters of the word being adopted for the sequence of grades for any particular year. It is an apt comment on the mystified state of English education when the word used is OBFUSCATION. If a child is born in the city of Leicester, he may go to either a grammar school, or more likely, a secondary modern school. If he is born just outside the city, he will go to a progressive comprehensive. Education is indeed 'just a chance he will have to take'. With such a system of educational differentials, the child, depending on his place of birth and childhood environment, could find himself in one of many varied school situations. But it is an education system based on such grading and differentials which can make whole sections of the population of Britain disbelieve in themselves as thinking, intellectual people with an active contribution to make in the government of their own lives. When a twelve-year old boy with a sharp intelligence and a deep concern for his future writes:

I am just a boy
    with a lot of dreams
but what's the point
    I won't get nowhere
I'm just ordinary
    nothing special just
        ordinary
got no chance in this
    world unless you're
        clever
which I'm not

Anonymous.

His sensitivity has plainly picked up the message of a society divided against him: 'Bad luck son, you haven't got it up top.' This is a message which a large proportion of the children of Britain, mostly in working class areas, soon receive. Others, born in a place where conditions will lead them towards academic progress and social opportunity, have different dreams, and go to different schools. For the unchosen and the unlucky, the dream is soon over:

> I hope not before the
> time I die I'll mash
> my dream to pieces.

14-year old boy.

For children with opportunities such as this boy had — trapped in a decaying, violent neighbourhood and a remove form at school, out of school at fifteen and into the Army, and steps toward Ulster — their schooling has not been a success in terms of education, but only in terms of mystification. It has meant that such children have accepted the grading and categories which a divided society forces on to them, as truths about themselves. They have accepted that some people have 'brains' and others do not, and it is these 'brains' which circumscribe anyone's chances in the world; that it is a man's 'brains' which determine a man's class and status:

> My future
> a millionaire to a tramp,
> what will be my future?
> It's limited to
> brains,
> and if I haven't got brains —
> a tramp
> a nightwatchman,
> no brains needed in those things.
> Or with brains a millionaire
> prime minister
> an executive.
> Brains —
> the gap between reality and tramps.

Jimmy, 11.

A system that is divided and hierarchical tells of its differentials and inequalities through its class system, the social crystallisation of its disrespect for people through its grading and categorising of them by class standards not applicable to them. When a working class boy aspires, he aspires to the standards heaved upon him at school, towards the middle class dream. The self-labelling which comes as a consequence of the failure of the dream when put next to the child's social reality, is an extension of the insults and disrespect a child receives through being graded by divided, hierarchical standards:

> I think I'll be an executive.
> That's what I think I'll be
> My Dad says I'll be on the bins,
> That's what he thinks of me.

Alan, 12.

Being on the bins in Widnes, or a tramp in Whitechapel, carries with it the lowest mark, the stigma of brainlessness. For the working class child, the middle class executive is right at the top of the class.

A working class child shouts of his own Identity, a shout for respect, to have his own ideas listened to and his own individuality developed in a democratic context:

One has to be explicitly political & doctrinaire to get this kind of response.

> Me, I'm just plain old me.
> But . . . I'm not plain I'm different
> to everyone else because
> they're not me, I'm me,
> I'm different to other people
> I talk different, I feel
> things different,
> I am different
> I have my own Identity.
> I have my own Ideas
> With what should be done with this world.

Tony, 15.

23

This is seen as something less important than his application to absorb facts and work towards inevitable examinations. Examinations can often splinter the emerging identity of the child and drive him towards a premature neurosis. At a time when the child should be confirming his identity, strengthening his feeling of belongingness to his world, and his class, and building up an integrated idea of himself in relationship to his world, his mind can be driven to nervous divisions, as even at the age of thirteen his education breaks up his mind:

> Three more years!
> My shaking hand will grasp my pen
> And frantically scribble.
> The sweat will flow as fast as ink
> In nervous desperation.
>
> Pass or fail?
> I'll scan the list to find my name,
> The worst I'll be expecting.
> Now will a college be my fate?
> Or National Assistance?

Jean, 13.

The child becomes divided against himself. The anticipation of his ordeal makes him see himself merely as a unit for successful or unsuccessful consumption by a society solely geared to examination results. His humanity is degraded, broken. The 'nervous desperation' to achieve adds to the confusion of adolescence. Like the teacher, the child quickly recognises and chases his career prospects and gets on with the job. He has no share in the government or decision-making in the life of his school. That is taken care of by other, higher, people. His education is not for participation or democracy, but for consumption. He will make profit for someone else, and a salary for himself. That is the vision of life school life offers him, and no matter how lovingly his teacher treats him, unless he committedly opposes this situation by political struggle in the schools, he is in absolute collusion with this future.

24

As the teacher competes amongst his colleagues for the graded posts and extra allowances, the child is also set against his peers in the fierce and 'healthy' competition of school life. In such a context, the building of a collective identity, of a co-operative, trusting group acting together and respecting and belonging to each other, becomes an anomaly and a threat. The usual confirmation of the 'group' is the confirmation of acting together in absurdity and frustration, being partners and objects in a shared disrespect and triviality: 'We are only "us", because of "them".' In this situation, the old enemies, prejudices and divisions are also re-affirmed:

[handwritten margin note: The only unit is rebellion.]

SCHOOL RULES

We're to sit and work
All day long we sit.
The pips go, We rise.
We leave. All regulated.

Steps out of place
We get told off
'Wear school uniform
Wear flesh-coloured tights'.

It's sickening how these things go
They never know what we think . . .

Sandra, 15.

This writer was a fourth-form school leaver, a highly intelligent and inquisitive girl. She got out of school as quickly as she could after her fifteenth birthday. She had had enough.

The 'divide and school' situation gives very little respect to parental contribution and participation. In some schools parental involvement is seen as parental interference. The idea of the teacher himself being in a position of 'locum parentis' over the children he teaches while they are at school, is one designed to exclude the child's real parents, and to ensure that the authority figure switches to the teacher while the child is inside the school walls. The idea of two sets of parents — teachers and mother and father — working together is seen as conflict, because for so much of the time the schools see their commission as compensating for or trying to mend the damage done by the home experiences and class background of the child. The schools have a continuous pretext for shifting the blame when their failures are becoming obvious. In the present truancy increase, the schools can always blame the situation on to the home life of the child, rather than look into their own insufficiencies. Speaking to a local paper, an East End Headmaster said:

> 'Truancy does exist. We know about it and
> often catch boys only a few yards away from
> the school. They climb over the back gate.
> We often find that there are family
> problems behind the persistant truant.'

A child's analysis of the problem may be very different from this:

> When does boredom start
> When does boredom stop
> From 9 till 4.30 the boredom goes on
> You can't wait till the end of the day
> To get out and do something you want
> Why are so many people bored with school?

Pat, 15.

The sense of boredom and incarceration that many children feel in an exploitative and consumptive school situation is far more relevant to the problem of truancy:

> You get freedom out of school
> And you get locked up in school
> just like a prison.
> The bell goes at ten to nine,

Five more minutes of freedom —
The bell has gone and I am bored.

Susan, 15.

But the schools will always use 'home problems' to ease their way out of their own problems. In a recent survey conducted by the Medical Research Council's Social Medicine Unit, it was revealed that in the East End of London, the single most important factor in determining whether a child becomes a 'delinquent' and appears before the courts, is the school he attends. Their research completely reversed the majority view very widely and conveniently held in the the schools that the home environment and lack of parental control is the determining factor in whether a child becomes a 'delinquent'. Dr. Michael Power, one of the researchers, said:

'Those children from schools with low
delinquency figures who did get into trouble
were much less likely to get in trouble a
second time than those at high delinquency
schools.'

The attitude of the schools was to withdraw permission for the unit to carry on with their research in the East End schools, and for a spokesman of the local education authority to say to the Press:

'This is not a reflection on those schools —
on the contrary, it is an indication that some
heads and their staff are prepared to accept
and do their best for what might be regarded
as more than their fair share of problem pupils.'

The 'problem' is seen as the pupils and their lives, not the state or nature of society and the schools. It is not that such pupils are 'maladjusted', it is that the society and schools are maladjusted to their human and social needs. They are 'maladjusted' to an affirmation of the working class.

The essential division made between home and school is heightened in a working class area, where the schools, surrounded by fences and walls, block themselves off from the community they pretend to serve.* The parents are allowed into the school by appointment, to meet the Head or the teacher in charge of the 'pastoral care' of his child. The teacher is in his office or the Head sits behind his desk. The parent, conscious of his own lack of official 'schooling' is faced with the professional man, the man of status who is 'responsible' for his child's education. This territory, he feels, is not his. The atmosphere, created by professional, outside people intimidates him. Sitting by himself, in these surroundings, facing the teacher, the parent is isolated. Even the token gestures made to parental participation in the London schools, where one parent is allowed onto the governing body of the schools, is made absurd when the rules of confidentiality do not allow the parent to report on official proceedings to his peers.

The schools, middle class units grafted onto a working class culture, become communities within themselves, existing not to reflect, affirm and strengthen local identity, but to break and stifle it. The parent's contribution becomes irrelevant and retrogressive to the schools' interest, to evangelise the top streams towards the middle class, and to drop the rest back into the labour force. Most teachers commute in the morning, do their job, and go home in the early evening. They are not neighbours to the parents, but outside people. The established divisions of class and role, the teacher, the man who 'educates', the parents, the people who maintain and 'look after' are re-affirmed. If the parents and schools unite, they unite depressingly often through the power and intimidation of the schools' hold on the parents against the child: the impact of reports, the fear of officialdom, the dangers of not 'keeping up':

* POLICE CALLED TO SCHOOL
HEAD BANS MUMS FROM PLAYGROUND.
. . . The mothers said that that morning Mrs. O'Keeffe "flew down the stairs" and told them to get out of the playground when they ignored the notice. After arguments police were called.

Front Page story, *East London Advertiser*, 24/11/72

28

THE TALL MAN WITH THE GREY HAIR

A knock comes at the door
A tall man
With grey hair
steps in.
'I understand,'
Says he
'You have not
been at school.'
Mum's face
Grew long and yellow,
'Havn't you'
Says she.
Her long boney hand
Came swiftly round my face
And the tears run
down my face.

Gillian, 15.

When a body becomes so divided against itself, it begins to
disintegrate. The 'school' as it was always known is disintegrating.
The old authoritarian structure where roles were tyrannical, but
where roles were very clear, is giving way to 'liberal education', where
the old controls and values are being discarded, relaxed and broken.
In the wake of this direction, there are no new political values, only
a vague hope that change and novelty itself, an 'open ended' process,
will lead to a new notion of education. In the meantime, the dole
queues lengthen, frustration and impatience at social disrespect
grows, and in the schools truancy and confusion are met by alternate
shouts to repress and put down, and to de-school. The wastage
continues, and children of dynamic, underdeveloped intelligence
continue to leave schools as soon as they can, their sensitivity
insulted by the schools' irrelevance and confusion. Growing,
thinking, working class energy turns sourly to cynicism and
frustration midway through the teens. And the schools carry on.

We must heal these divisions in schools, as in all of society. We
must come together with new values, democratic socialist values,

values of participation and mutual respect. We will have to struggle in the schools, as we will everywhere. These divisions keep some people strong, and they will want to hold onto them. We must break them down, but first we must break down the walls between each other: teachers, children, parents. We must all be workers and neighbours, all contributing, all participating, all respecting, all solidarising. Only then can we oppose a vicious social machine whose every move is to divide and sectionalise.

BELONGINGNESS

East End
What is it
Dirt? Old buildings?

no-one is sure
The only thing I'm sure about
Is that I live there
and have done all my life . . .

The East End is like
Five parts of the world
put into one place.

Janice, 14.

Where I live, there are a lot of skinheads who sometimes
beat people up. If you have a fight with one of them and you
beat him, he will go and get his mates to beat you up.

There are three parts to my buildings, one part in Wicker St.
and the other two parts are in Langdale St.

On the corner of my street there is an old clothes shop
called 'Hettie's', and next to that there is a chicken shop where
they kill chickens.

At night all the rats from the two shops run to the old ruins,
but hardly any of them get there because of the cats.

The funniest thing I have ever seen was, one day one of the
men from the chicken shop was carrying in some chickens,
when one of them got away and the chicken started to fly and
the man was running in the road jumping up and down trying

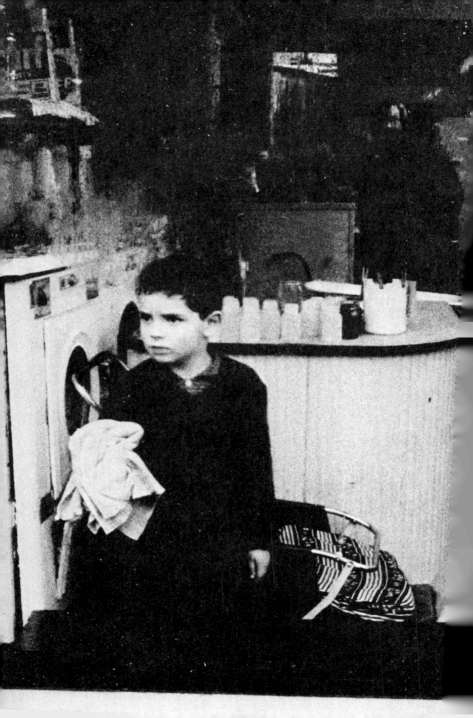

to get it. Nearly all the people in my building are old and Jewish. Really I wouldn't like to move away from my district because I know a lot of people there. Some people think that Stepney people are rough and a load of tramps, but they're not. They're just brought up in quite a tough part.

Peter, 11.

A working class child's identity inevitably involves the connection which he feels between himself and the place where he lives, the people, the buildings, the streets, the way and pace of life. He may be made secure or insecure by the feeling either of belonging or rejection he has for that place. Outside the circle of his immediate family to which he belongs, is the wider family of the local community. As he grows, he grows into definite attitudes towards this place and its people. He may grow to know very clearly its problems, yet still fell great affection and belonging for it:

STEPNEY

I think Stepney is a very smokey place
But I like it
People in Stepney do things wrong
But I like them
Everything in Stepney has its disadvantages
But I like it

It does not have clean air like the country
But I like it
The buildings are old and cold
But I like them
The summer is not very hot
But I like it.

Rosemarie, 12.

Or he may grow to hate and distrust this place and the people it seems to condition:

STEPNEY

I come from Stepney, lived there all me life
Loads of cheap markets
Bargains at half price
Jumpers,and skirts, trousers cheap
All muddled up in any old heap.

Dirty old women, shouting out their wares
Everybody stinks, nobody cares
All dirty, greasy things bunged into bins
Stinkin' rotten hole is Stepney.

                                        Diane, 12.

He may feel angry and alienated from this place where he has been
compelled by circumstances to live, and to continue to live:

We've just moved to Mile End
Where markets are dirty, the air is musty,
And all the stalls and shops are rusty.

Every night while watching tele
Police go racing by.
Sirens noisy, children scream . . .

                                        Pauline, 12.

He may even recognise that it is this place itself that is directing his
life, laying down the conditions of his unhappiness:

BRICK LANE

Brick Lane is a horrible place
Where everyone has a gloomy face
There isn't even one little space to play football
Everyone plays in the dirt

Filling their hair with dirt
What a place
I always try to be happy and cheerful
Now I begin to get doubtful.

Tony, 14.

A happy childhood involves a feeling of social health, feeling good
in a place which you love and which somehow seems to give love
back. If this place is a distinct community to which the child feels he
belongs, the connection will be a much more loyal one. Consequently
the eventual separation from the place which has become a part of
the emerging identity of the child, can be an uneasy and perplexing
experience:

WAPPING

I have lived in Wapping all my life,
It was such a friendly place.
Everyone knew everyone else,
or if you didn't you knew their face.

Me and my friends, used to
go down on the shores of
the River Thames in the mud
the dirt and stones,
We'd see the Police Boats going by,
O, such happy days.

Wapping is like a little island,
If you wanted to go to
Shadwell, or the other side of
Wapping,
You had to cross a bridge.

I used to live in Wapping,
but now I live in a different place,
. . . Stepney.

Carol, 12.

In the shuffling between two communities, like the older city environment and the new estate, the working class child's sense of belonging to his particular world — responsible as it is for framing much of his experience and identity, can feel strange and dislocated:

I moved to a place called Stepney
From Romford where I had been Happy.
I was quite lonely at first,
But I made some friends
And it wasn't at all bad
The house was cold, then in the night it was warm.

Days passed slowly, now they go quite fast.
It's not really bad
And I'm used to it,
But I long for the day when I go from this place.

I went down there this summer,
It seemed really quiet.
A lot of people still knew me
And I had a cup of tea in Harold Hill.
But it seemed quiet there
I felt uneasy there,
I got on the train home, and I felt that I could cry.

I got home, I was glad to be home
But I was glad I had been.
There are quite a few differences
But still I'd like to leave.

Anon, 13.

When working class children enter a school in their area, they are often told that they are entering into a new 'community': the 'community' of the school. A new sense of belonging is engendered into the children: they are part of a new community, and loyalty to that community is the touchstone of respect and success within it.

As a Deputy Headmistress of an East London 'Comprehensive' School said recently:

> 'As I see it, a school is a community, and it takes
> a long time to build it up, and a lot of co-operative
> effort. Just as in a family, if parents are at logger-
> heads and always at sixes and sevens, it is the
> children who suffer, so it is, I feel, in a
> school context where, if the staff are at
> loggerheads, again, it is the children who suffer.'

A separate community, or 'family' has been created within the already existing community where the child lives, and the child is introduced to the new standards, new loyalties of the new 'community'. The new community is the school, and the child must belong to it: his attendance is required compulsorily. The schools create a new area of belonging that is imposed upon the child. It is the belonging to the white middle class consciousness, and it is that consciousness which exists to break and divide the child's working class identity. The school becomes a white middle class transplant, inculcating a new and false notion of belonging to the working class child: a new culture of unbelonging. The child now 'belongs' to this new separate community, rather than to the local community. This new school community works hard to build up its credibility and prestige to the child's future employers, not the child's own working class world and identity.

Consequently, such children at school are seen largely as digits of variously categorised value who are either capable of preserving the level of the school's good name and status, or who are set aside as "non examination" and mostly assessed on the criterion of whether they are quiet and well behaved, or whether they speak too much. The right of the child to develop and exercise his own separate existence is seen to be less important than a quiet general atmosphere of 'good order'. In this situation the social being of the child is largely ignored as being inferior to the imposed frame of social values that are heaved over the child by his teachers. The child is coerced by a world that is not his own, that does not accept his own personal existence and social situation as important, and so his true potentialities of personal growth and social belongingness are

37

blocked. His true social situation may be shunned as retrogressive to the main criteria and directions of the school: to prepare a child for his future employers. A fourth form 'business studies' department is seen as a factory for producing girl secretaries and 'temps' to be supplied for the consumption and use of city business. So a 'school bank' in the 'business studies' department of the school, is seen as a prestigious element of school life: it impresses the girls' future employers, and may lead the girls towards a more glamorous city office. The Deputy Headmistress speaks again:

> 'The bank is quite unique, I gather, and something of
> a showpiece. We frequently have visitors, and it is,
> of course, run by the youngsters themselves. This
> was, I believe, in the Daily Telegraph. This is an
> achievement of which the youngsters are very proud,
> and of which the school is very proud.'

The breaking of children's working class collective identities at school through the offensive of the middle class consciousness, is only accompanying a general destruction of working class, neighbourhood life. When the place that a child belongs to is being demolished and broken apart, his identity becomes uncertain, his relationship to his foundering neighbourhood begins to give him only insecurity. His world is changing around him, and he becomes unsure, unbalanced and very vulnerable. A new world of concrete and glass blocks, isolated high rise flats and neat maisonettes is replacing the old streets and neighbours:

> I live in a block of tall flats, but I only live on
> the second floor. I used to live down a street where
> everyone knew each other, and you could open the
> street doors if it was warm. We moved into flats four
> years ago, there very nice flats with big rooms, but
> I'd give anything to live down the old street with
> the same people. I used to know everyone and my mum
> used to talk to everyone who she knew. But now we live
> on a landing with four people and the landings are

Our kids have never had this ,

38

closed in and I don't know two of the people. I don't
know why but I don't like it in a flat. We haven't even
got a balcony where we can sit in the sun.

We had to move out of the same block opposite because
the flats wasn't safe. There are three blocks all the
same. We are in the middle one now. Down my old street
I used to stand at the door but I can't now instead I
stand and look out the window.

We used to moan about the old houses but if you ask any
one of the people who lived there, they would say they
would rather live back there.

But now there all knocked down and flats are being built
there and four of the people who used to live there who
I knew are dead.

Jenny, 14.

At this time, when the child is in a shifting, fluctuating state, the
old props of his previous way of life are no longer holding secure.
His old standards and symbols no longer serve. And at this stage the
school 'community' with its more consistent and methodical middle
class norms and standards begins to exert its influence with the child
and becomes particularly persuasive. Thus the collusion between the
physical break-up and demolition of a working class area, and the
existential breakdown of a child's old working class identity is
cleverly synchronised and managed. The child grasps on to the
middle class way, although he may have no roots there. He becomes
divided, confused, alienated from his old life. His own culture has
seemed to collapse around him, destroyed by what his middle class
teachers may tell him is 'progress'. His imagery and symbols,
previously in the streets and life around him, (*'My streets are my
ideas for my Imagination'*, BLAKE) which told him of his identity
and belonging, lie broken amongst the rubble of demolition or
scattered on the derelict sites, swept behind the hoardings. The
wilderness and devastation of the all-but-demolished Scotland Road
area of Liverpool has also meant the destruction of the identity of
the community of people who lived there, and everything which
kept it unique and strong for its citizens. Bill Murphy, one of the
founders of the Scotland Road Free School, has said how he feels

40

the people there have been robbed of the strength and security of their own identity:

'If they have no identity and no standards by which to make comparisons, they can't really gain anything from anyone else, certainly not through books. You need you own imagery. If you have no imagery, or if it has been destroyed, what kind of richness can you get from Shakespeare? If you can't formulate anything in your own mind, how can you take from the richness of the culture?'

The Free School itself exists as a part of a much broader movement to revitalise the old identity, to re-charge it, and make it strong and formidable again:

'We're concerned about all the people here picking themselves up and saying NO, and getting them involved in their own area — the planning of their own area, and making it a place that is worth living in.'

The state schools in working class areas must also give children confirmation and support in their own identity, and not break it to pieces. The same process which is happening to the black child in England is also happening to the white working class child: the white middle class consciousness is assaulting the identity of them both, and is the enemy of them both. At a period of time when the fragmentation of the old neighbourhood life in the inner-city is so intense, when vast new estates, tower blocks, motorways and flyovers, giant comprehensive schools and shopping centres are disfiguring and obliterating old, smaller communities, mechanising and speeding up the lives of the people — old identities are crumbling, foundering. New people move into areas of decay for different motives: sometimes immigrant groups, relieved at the cheaper rent and multiple occupation of a run-down area, sometimes

41

more prosperous middle class people, pleased with an old Georgian terrace house to make elegant and fashionable again, and live there in genteel splendour. In this social context, the children of the old working class community are unsettled, anxious, wondering where they fit in. They, and their families, are often in a dilemma: where is their world? Is it still in their old, crumbled, dislocated community, or is it a new life in a new town somewhere, away from the violence and confusion of upheaval:

> I have lived in my house for 13 years. My parents were brought up in Limehouse, and so was my eldest sister and brother. They sometimes tell me how much it has changed since they went to school, my sisters, brothers, parents. But I can see for myself what has really changed around my area. Our slums. There was a time when I could go anywhere I wanted to. School was just across the road. There was no trouble going to school of a morning and coming home at night. But then my old friends changed with the change of school. My friends moved away. Other people moved in. People with children who loved trouble. Who live in trouble and want to make more and more. I can remember mods and rockers, now it is Pakistanis, mainly the coloured people cause trouble. The skinheads, the greasers. I don't mix with any of the people around my area. I can't make a conversation. I don't make any friends from my area. I just stay indoors. When I do finally go out with some little girls of eight or nine, I do meet some boys I used to hang around with, who would bother to talk to me. But then that's that. They have made new friends since. Our area stinks. It is not a nice area. No trees, or beautiful flowers in gardens, nothing. It is not clean. The houses are falling to pieces with familes of 13. The coloured people are making use of these, but have 5 different families to one small house. In some areas a white person is nowhere to be seen. Just groups of ten coloured people, everywhere.
> But I am determined to make new friends when I

move to Milton Keynes, Bletchley, This is a
beautiful town. All the houses, all the stairs —
a dream we have all wanted in our family, are new
and even now being built. They are modern, and
the small pathways leading to different houses are
clean. There are fields, small streams, full of
cows, sheep, horses, flowers. There are no high sky-
scrapers, and no flats. I can imagine looking out of
my bedroom window, and just seeing fields and horses,
and not smoke, filth, high buildings, hardly no sky
that's what you would call clear. No trouble. Where
I will be accepted as a friend. Will find a good job,
live and have my children, far away from Stepney.

Maxine, 13.

The swallowing up of small communities inside a large city into
larger urban units very often involves a shift away from an organic,
communal life where people meet and talk and jostle in the streets,
and live close enough to each other not to need cars. The move may
be to a far less pedestrian and more mechanised, impersonalised
existence where larger, more convenient but less socialising influences
are becoming increasingly powerful. This can be seen in obvious
daily routines like shopping. The small street market, like Watney
Street in Stepney, dies away. The impressions the child feels here are
warm, full of humour and affectionate detail; of people involved in
close human contact on the street:

WATNEY STREET

Chattering, talking holding up the traffic.
Women shopping buying fruit, food
on the outlook for a bargain.
Man on the corner selling stolen purses
one eye on the cash box
one eye on the look out
fruit seller shouting 'buncha bananas',
Someone buys, some don't know they're half rotten

One selling toys made in Hong Kong.
Old men under the arch selling broken plates.

Alan, 12.

Here the person is more important than the machine, the shoppers stop the cars in the street. But the street market is gradually being replaced by the new, machine-like supermarket. A child very soon notices the different atmosphere, the different quality of life which this kind of shopping generates: where people don't seem to want to talk but only queue and complain and become impatient: where the shopper moves through the stacks and shelves of food as if he is on a conveyor belt and serves himself without human touch or conversation: where the child feels unhappy and threatened among the brittle tempers:

THE SUPERMARKET

I managed to squeeze through the door
And greet the hot, bustling crowd which awaited me.
It's as though I were squeezed into a small
                              sardine tin.
I reached for a tin of peas
And found the whole lot rushing at my feet —
I moved on, trying not to crash against the wall,
Everyone seems in a hurry
As though the world were to end in five minutes.
I finally managed to get my few bits and pieces together,
And now the wait,
The wait that really depresses,
That really tenses my nerves.
I stand lonely, uneasy —
The line moves,
I relax my muscles and fight to keep my place
As a fat lady snatches at a packet of Cadbury's Smash,
And another lady lashes out furiously at a small child
Who pesters her for an ice-lolly.
Once again the line moves.

And I move too.
A wasp stings an assistant —
This holds up the line even more.
I wait, now annoyed and still depressed.
I wait for ten minutes.
The assistant finally comes back,
Her arm clumsily bandaged.
I await my turn . . .
At last it comes.
I put my bits on the counter —
She tried to reckon up my things,
She reached for a bottle of orange squash
But knocked it on the floor
Causing an even longer delay.
At last my chance came
To greet the fresh air once again.
I rush to the door,
A refreshing breeze greets me —
Everything so different
So calm, so free.

Ramona, 11.

What seems important is the conclusion that a child not only feels
better if he knows and likes the place where he lives, but also feels
that this place is not too big, not impersonal and indifferent or
hostile to him, or not too fast. If he feels that he can circumscribe
the world he knows, know both its extent and its boundaries and
sense its social warmth and concern, then he may grow into a
stronger feeling of belonging for it. In a faster, mechanised place that
has lost its distinctness and identity, the child may feel left behind
and alienated; that the world where he lives is not his:

THEIR WORLD

People they are always rushing about,
driving, walking, running,
It's always the same,

nobody stops to think about
    themselves, their world.

Perhaps its instinct
Perhaps its the stink of the dustbins,
They just hurry on not a
minute to spare,
If they hurry on any more they
    just won't be there.
People they are always on the run
But will they look round and
    see what they have done?

Carol, 12.

When a child feels good in his own community, that community
can expand in his mind and become the whole world. The feeling of
people together, a united working class, living in a place which offers
them contact and connection with each other, becomes a feeling of
social love and one-ness; and a position of potential political strength.
The child has achieved a position of security in his own world, with
his own people, his own class. He knows that he belongs, and he has
a base worth preserving, improving, and fighting for:

A TRIP TO SHADWELL PARK

The cool gentle breeze that moves the ripples of water
    and causes it to crash against the concrete wall
The barges never going anywhere just continue to sway from
    side to side like they are nailed to the bottom
Distant shouts from passengers aboard a pleasure cruiser
The droppings of sweets and crisps, luring pigeons
Old people with nothing to do, watching the action
Small children, too young to go to school, amuse themselves
    by running round, exploring, investigating things
The friendly people, amongst them an old woman ridden to a
    wheelchair
A man with his camera giving us hints on our camera

An old frame of a pram stuck in the mud with water flowing
    over it
The smells
Refreshing smells
The river, with a mixture of smells
Oil and sewerage
Small patches of flowers giving a mild scent to the air
Two Pakistani women and a baby, neglected, unattended,
    talking their way, keeping themselves to themselves
Would the park and its people let them in on the act?
And the old woman
The old Jewish woman, wishing for her childhood back —
To think that we were giving her so much pleasure.
Birds hovering above the picture
The lifelike picture
Everyone taking part
A man unaware of everthing, in a deep sleep
Stretched out on a bench
People everywhere, on their own or with friends, enjoying
    the beautiful weather.

Sharon, 11

'A Trip to Shadwell Park' is a picture of integrated life, of a working class community interacting within itself, the people flowing into each other, into the surroundings, and even those surroundings themselves, the flowers, the river, the birds — giving back a sense of love and belonging. A few months after the poem was written, the park was threatened by a plan to erect a Heliport in the vacant, derelict dock entrance next to the park. The Heliport was to be used as a means of quick and convenient access and exit to and from city offices by city businessmen. Shadwell is then only five minutes away from the centre of the City of London. This would have destroyed the park as a focal centre for the local community. It was another example of an outside, exploiting, mechanistic force breaking and spoiling a facility which brought together different age and racial groups and individuals living locally, and gave them the initiative to jill and harmonise. Then came the threat of noise, danger, pollution all from outside, to disturb and break up a working, inter-relating community. The Heliport, it was argued, was proof of progress, and would add prestige and excitement to the East End of London. Many people living in Shadwell and Wapping fought and organised against the idea, recognising the further exploitation and discomfort it would create. Two twelve year old boys wrote poems on the issue which were read out to the inspector from the Ministry of Environment by another boy at the public enquiry on the Heliport:

THE HELIPORT

No to the Heliport
We all can do without it
They've shut the docks
And now look what we've got —
A noisy bloody object.

No to the heliport
That's what we all say
What do we get out of it?
Nothing but noise all day.

No to the heliport
We must all shout together
We'll keep our buses, trains and planes
But helicopters — we can do without 'em.

Timmy, 12.

We don't want your helicopters
Can't use 'em.
We don't want your helicopters
Can't fly 'em.

We'll keep what we've got —
Noise which shakes old buildings
We don't want.
We don't want your heliport
So send it back.

What a noise, what smoke —
Pollute some other area
Keep your heliport out.

Eli, 12.

The boys recognised the threat of the Heliport, and its potential
for destroying a part of their world. For them, their educational
experience with the Heliport had been actional. With other
neighbours they had joined in the fight to save a part of their own
world, a part of their own identity, and the meeting place for old
people resting by the river, or young mothers wheeling their babies
in the only local park on a sunny afternoon. *

It was a typical issue in which the local schools should have been
involved. In Scotland Road, over a similar issue, the Free School
would have been there, adding their weight to the reclaiming of their
identity, fighting for their area. As Bill Murphy said: 'The whole of
Liverpool is our classroom. In Liverpool, wherever anything's
happening, we're there — we go there.' The role of the schools
should not be to stand aside when the children's and parents' world
is threatened, or to betray the children by robbing them of their
working class identities by the gradual imposition of middle class
standards and attitudes which will divide and alienate them. The
schools should promote and affirm the identity of their students. If
the teachers also were fellow neighbours and workers with the
children and their parents, they would have been fighting against the
Heliport too, and any such incursion upon their common, mutual
world. Then the teachers' own area of life would have been similarly
involved. They would have found themselves acting along with the
children and their parents, and not against them in the divided,
contesting situation of present school life. They would have had and
enjoyed reciprocity, comradeship, shared experience. An actional
education is such an experience, where people break down the walls

* As a local resident said at the Public Enquiry: 'We're not having
Shadwell and Wapping used as a doormat for city businessmen to
wipe their dirty feet on before stepping into their city offices.'
Due to pressure from local rank and file, the 'Heliport' project was
abandoned.

between them and live and fight together to preserve, expand and discover what is theirs, to affirm their class, their neighbourhood, their world, and their own sense of belonging to each other:

'To educate man to be ACTIONAL, preserving
in all his relations his respect for the
basic values that constitute a human world,
is the prime task of him,who, having taken
thought, prepares to act.' *

Frantz Fanon.

*Black Skins, White Masks, p.158 (*Paladin Books*)

NEIGHBOURS

THE MAN

There was a man in the street,
So old and cold he could not speak,
With eyes of blue and hair of grey
He walked and walked by, did not speak.

He walked through the day,
He walked by night,
With clothes so old with holes,
So if you see this man, help him
    if you can.

Beverly, 12.

' . . . *revolutionary activity is really* human *empathetic,
loving, communicative and humble, in order to be liberating.*'

Paulo Freire. *

   The function of the teacher of English in a working class area is
to promote respect amongst people and to strengthen and affirm the
identity of those people. Those people, in the school situation,
should be his neighbours: children, parents and other teachers. His
job is to work to break down the divisions between these groups, and
to work towards a unity and one-ness in his neighbourhood whereby

* Paulo Freire *Pedagogy of the Oppressed*, p. 139. (*Penguin, 1972*) .

51

the people there, including himself, move to gain more control and participation in the conditions and decisions governing their own lives. His job, in short, is to promote democracy. Literacy and literature are then seen in this prior context: of serving people and creating intellectual confidence and self-respect amongst working class children, bringing them to an awareness of their social situation in a class-based society through the spoken and written word, and affirming the collective strength of their class:

> All living in one community
> Thinking for each other
> Helping each other
> No betrayals . . .

> Maxine, 13.

The English teacher in the schools is probably in the best position to give back to the child his own world and identity in his education, to re-affirm it, to share it himself, support it and strengthen it. This emphasis can only be credible to both the child and teacher if they are both neighbours, if they live close to each other and share the same life-experiences: if they walk down the same streets, use the same parks, if the teachers and parents talk and drink in the same pubs. In this way, the walls surrounding the schools are knocked down, and the entire neighbourhood world becomes the classroom.

In the act of recognition of their own area in a distinct art form, children begin to rediscover and re-think their world. By giving them back their world, for example in a series of photographs illustrating the people and streets which they know and live amongst, a new starting point can be created in their instinctive relationship with their world. Suddenly they are confronted with their neighbourhood in a new way, and the response of recognition generates a new creative energy. The child points to the photographs, and writes:

I know this place
I know it well,
I sometimes go past, stop and dwell
I hear the people
I see the people,
Talking, chating, smileing
Walking
Their is a pub just down the road
A school at the back
And a youth centre
That doesent lack

Tony, 13.

This world which the child recognises around him is a world full of images, symbols, rhythms, shapes. His streets, full of people and buildings, are also full of poetry and drama. With poetry and drama, his English education becomes actional. Children writing plays about their world together, writing in groups, pooling their ideas to reproduce the drama of the neighbourhood, affirm both their individual and collective identities. Poetry itself becomes an immense socialising force, bringing people together. The great power that poetry gives is the power of imaginative empathy, to share the lives of other people and become them, to inspire and create a unity and one-ness. In this sense, poetry becomes the most political of actions, a moving outward of the individual consciousness to find new forms and new people, to explore, discover and change the world.

It is the people and streets in a child's life that help him to forge out his images of identity. He begins to see his own life in terms of his immediate surroundings, his own world. As he asks questions about himself, and who he is, it is his neighbours and environment that may give him his answers and knowledge, not the facts chosen for him by a different consciousness at his school. His poem may be a shout of his own identity, and his life in his community with his peers becomes important in the development of a collective identity for the child and his friends. Poetry is an immediate way of expressing this collective experience of childhood:

WHAT DO THEY FEEL?

What do they feel
those little kids
running and jumping in the streets
playing run outs
or knocking on doors
what do they feel
rolling on the floors?
In the country, or on Mars
do they play the same as those?

Caroline, 11.

The imaginative act of poetry, discovery with words and images,
parallels the exploratory activity of play, which educates while it
satisfies, whether over an adventure playground or derelict site:

THE ROLLING ROPE

As you run up the ramp
You've got to be fast
Or else you'll slide back down again.
When you get to the top, you can see the tops
    of the people's heads,
Then you walk along a thin, half-burnt log —
You've got to be careful or else you'll fall off.
Then you come to the rope
    the rolling rope
Somebody swings it up
You grab hold of it
Then you jolt
You're on, you're on the rolling rope,
You feel like Tarzan falling through the trees.
You look at the post
It's coming nearer and nearer
You think you're going to crash,
But the rolling rope is slowing down

As if it knows you're in danger . . .
Then it stops.
You get off and start again.

David, 11.

EMPTY DOCKS

I go to a raft
it is so big and fat
it floats on water
and moves like a rat

It is in the ghostly docks
it's made of solid wood
from the gates of the locks —
I go in the daytime and in the night

I go with my mates
We climb the big gates
to get on this big fat raft
And then we row out and about

We cross the water
from side to side
We heave with sticks
in a heavy great stride

We know we will cross
to see the moss
on each side
of the rocky docks

Gary, 14

The use of accepted rhythms and rhyme structures which are
commonly known can be used to create new, contemporary
experience in a contemporary, ballad-like form. This is done

collectively and massively by football crowds, but it can also happen individually, when a boy wants to make his own critical comment on the activities of his peers:

HOOLIGANISM

Ten little football fans
Making rude signs,
One swore at a policeman
Then there were nine.

Nine little football fans
Stirring up some hate,
One got bottled
And then there were eight.

Eight little football fans
The youngest was eleven,
He smashed up a buffet
And then there were seven.

Seven little football fans
Hitting people with sticks,
One tried to fight alone
And then there were six.

Six little football fans
Playing with a knife,
One got stabbed
Then there were five.

Five little football fans
One fell on the floor,
He got crushed
And then there were four.

Four little football fans
Just like you and me,
One threw a penny at the goalie
Then there were three.

Three little football fans
The other team did boo,
But the fans outnumbered them
Then there were two.

Two little football fans
After all was done
One ran on the football pitch
Then there was one.

One little football fan
Glad his team had won,
Argued with some other fans
Then there were none.

Peter, 14.

And the actual exercise of poetry itself, in pushing out the
consciousness towards another in the act of empathy, can create and
confirm connection and friendship when young people write about
themselves and their world:

OURSELVES BY US

We sit next to each other in school
of a night we go around the garage
to our gang of Greecers
one of us never goes anywhere without the
other
unless we have to.
    We always share our things
    with each other
    We argue about things
    But we always stay friends.
    We go to the same Cave
    And we both go to the same Cafe.

Gillian and Vicki, 14.

Poetry can also cause important communication within the home. It can express an assertion and confirmation of respect and love from child to parent, when conditions are hard and the family is struggling:

MIRACLES

Mum, if I could work miracles,
I would work one just for you,
We know you've worked hard
To bring us up right —
That's for sure,
What with Daddy being sick
We have been very poor,

But still we are happy
Despite the dismal gloom
But God knows there will come a time
When we all shall feel the . . .
    BOOM

                              Tony, 14.

Or it can stimulate a parent's own reflection of the same struggle:

Life isn't funny
Without any money.

It's a bitter end
Without a friend.

It wasn't so bad
When I was young and gay.

But it's a different story.
Now I'm old and grey.

                              Julie.

The conflicts at home can sometimes be expressed through poetry, and much of the bitterness removed. When the parents of this poet saw what she had written, it stimulated discussion and communication about the relationships within that family:

My mother defies me, my father defies me,
Yet, I feel mixed up.
The only friends I'll ever have
Are bullies in the making.

I tell my mum their harmless,
their only having fun,
they say 'Live while you're younger,
Causing trouble is no danger'
Not while you've legs to run.

I like their kind of living,
It's free, and no one takes no notice
of us, they just feel disgusted
at the younger generation
I like the feeling of not being stared at
I like the carefree feeling

Maxine, 13.

Two weeks later, the same girl wrote a poem which confirmed her understanding of the pressures on her family and the love of her parents. The complexities of her family life had been confronted, and she had a different and more positive statement to make: that family life in a decaying and violent working class area like Spitalfields in East London is full of desperate contradictions, beyond the individual control of her parents:

They don't understand,
they think my parents are strict,
they are stupid,
because I am in at nine each night,
and shouted at a lot,

I think it is better, it is better
for me, if only they could see.
They think they are martyrs, their
children are hooligans,
and they could not care less.
They still call themselves mothers,
They children come in what time
they like, steal from shops, what
they like, they show they are big,
to youngers, and the old.
Big!! eh!
As big as my little toe, no doubt.
They, those parents, accuse
my mother of cruelty.
Cruelty is best, and anyway
I am hardly ever hit,
The mothers' and fathers' language
is disgraceful, their
behaviour is disgusting, in the
pub, mother at bingo, Father?
'He is down at the betting shop again.'
They don't feel sorry for themselves,
they feel sorry for me,
Jesus Christ, I have more pity
for them, than for Oxfam, or Biafra.
They don't realise I love my parents
more than anything else that may
be dear to me. I am happy. More
so happy than they could be.
Because I know they love me.
They do all these things, that
they think are awfull, which are not
really, because they care for me.
They do it all for me.
They love me.
and, I love them.
I'm thankful, and I will be in the future.

Just as a child may see her identity in terms of a neighbourhood environment that gives her a feeling of health and hope, so she may also see this sense of belonging strengthened in her home, amongst her family. And the words can flow with the confidence she feels in her family:

> Inside my cobweb mind there's a gap, an opening
> Where my secrets are keeping away from the world.
> I wonder sometimes how my dreams are kept inside,
> One by one they are let out to tell me of my
>   life and love.
> But my heart is sometimes lonely and waiting to
>   be opened by the key, the key of my heart.
> But my outside is clean where I wash everyday,
>   but my hair, what a mess!
> My teeth are sometimes dirty, and my hands
>   are sometimes too.
> I am short and ugly, sleepy too,
> And my saying is 'Good things come in
>   small packets'.
> My mum and dad love me.
> I know that is true because my mum gives me dinners
>   and her love everyday,
> And my dad gives me money and his love everyday.
> I have two brothers, lovely they are (what a lie)
> But that's not true
> I care for my brothers, and they care
>   for me too.
>
> Lesley, 11.

The exercise of imaginative empathy is a daily activity. In a pedestrian society where people still walk around the streets, they look at other people and may stop and talk and exchange ideas. They may also think and wonder about the people they see and try to project themselves inside them to try to understand their thoughts and problems. This in itself is empathy — an exchange of minds, people, however temporarily, considering and becoming the person they are contemplating. Once they have thought this way about another person, the barriers are broken and a connection has been made, a bridge has been built over a void. Poetry can be such a bridge, as the child considers the people she sees in the streets around her, and wonders about their life-situations and experiences:

THINKING

Looking at people
Thinking what they are thinking,
Is it troubles she or he is thinking about,
or is it children?
Maybe it's a drunken husband,
is she thinking 'What nice people'.
Or how right they are or wicked
and how the children look.
or is she thinking 'I wonder how my
children are.'
Or the men thinking 'Is my wife left me
or is she in the pub as usual.'
NO ONE knows
NO ONE WANTS to know.

Marion, 11.

In the claustrophobic environment of a great city, there may be a special kind of loneliness, where people are so much smaller than the brick and concrete around them. In this situation, communication with each other and the exercise of empathy becomes vital:

THE LONELY ROAD TO EDUCATION

Out into the open air to the fresh
atmosphere.
Everyone neatly dressed,
Working men, school kids.
None talking to each other.
Just the clip clop of the heels
clashing against the hard ground

and their alternate dips into the
puddles left by the night rain.
Everyone trying to occupy themselves
but no one speaks.
Out into the open air into the fresh
atmosphere.
For a quiet walk to school.

Sharon, 11.

This empathy becomes even more necessary in a society which is becoming more and more mechanised. Empathy becomes the starting point of compassion, and its direction is nowhere more important than towards the old, the unfortunate, the rejected and the victimised. By writing poetry and extending themselves imaginatively towards these people, children begin to understand their situation more, and their plight and problems. Once the mind has entered another, its attitude completely changes towards that other. So that children, young and growing, begin to understand the isolation and loneliness of age, and they can begin to break it down:

I am old and frightened
in this darkened world
I'm shut behind bars
Still, I've had my day . . .

Yes I remember when I was a girl
with fancy clothes and a man by my side,
He has gone now, he was a man,
    a great man,

He's left me now
it will be my day soon.
Here today and gone tomorrow.

Margaret, 12.

THERE ARE LOTS of OLD WOMEN
    MEN AS Well
All Sitting in Rooms and
Looking at well

THAY wonder if they Shall
See the world or even
See the Sky as well

THAY moan, they groan
THAY Sit and cry some times
THAY think they're going to die.

        G. MATTHEW

REST

I'm old
I need rest
maybe it's the gardening I do
maybe the long walk I take
maybe it's in my mind.
At night in bed I rejoice at the rest
I'm having.
My muscles are getting stiff
Sometime I get rheumatism in my legs
I'm getting very old I need rest

Jimmy, 11

MY COLD, OLD HOUSE

I live on my own
In a cold damp room
No-one to talk to,
No-one to see.

My children are married
They live far away
My husband died
On a cold winter's day.

I feel oh so lonely
I feel oh so sad
The only company I have is my tom cat,
He's a lovely little cat.

Tina, 12.

An old man stands outside his old shop like a shack
Where he sells his time pieces
Wall clocks
Wrist watches

Any piece of time
He's old and his time probably up
It can't be put back
Maybe in some other time and place
Time won't matter any more.

Pat, 15.

And the cycle is made complete when old people begin to move
backwards to understand and remember their own childhood and its
sensations. With children moving towards the old, and the old
moving towards childhood again, the age barriers can be lifted away
through the act of poetry. Here, a pensioner remembers her own
childhood in Stepney, and the sense of release and exhilaration of a
trip to Greenwich:

REMEMBERING

Hop, skip, jump!
Just one mile to Aldgate Pump;

Stride along to London Bridge.
Board the steamer —
Here we go
Down the river —
Oh, so slow.

There's the tower
All white and square.

Under Tower Bridge
and through the 'Pool'.

Pass the docks
and see the boats.
Bring tea and spices from afar.

Then Heigh ho! to Greenwich Pier

Disembark and you are there.

Run to the park across the road,
Race up the hill —
It's all puff and blow.

Look back and see the wondrous sight,
River, boats, Palace,
Shining bright.

The evening sun glows soft and red —
    And I just sit — Remembering.

                                        Milly Harris, 65.

In an area with a high population of vagrants and dossers, like the
East End of London, the word 'tramp' does not carry with it a great
deal of sympathy:

TRAMPS

Tramps, tramps that's all we get in Stepney now
they drink all night and sleep all day
they don't go to work
they don't like work

They smell of drink and
smell of beer
they lay in the dirt to drink
there beer

They don't have a wash
They don't have a bath
they just sleep where they can,
they sometimes have some meths.

                                        Boy, 12.

Whitechapel and Spitalfields is both a refuge and an asylum for the homeless and socially rejected, and children there grow up with them on the same streets. There is a simultaneous acceptance and rejection, pity and abhorrence towards them. An acceptance of a homeless, ragged dosser is an acceptance of Man completely, of the real 'bare fork'd animal'. When children accept such a man through their poetry, they have acquired a very basic and profound knowledge and understanding of the nature and mortality of man. Such an acceptance promotes a strong levelling effect:

> I am a homeless man, I sleep in a Savation Army
> Hostel. I play the mouth organ to make a few coppers
> so I can by a bit of tobacco. I have nothing to live
> for, I just live day by day. Skinheads and young
> people laugh at me and take the mickey but I am past
> worrying and I just don't care anymore. They forget
> they will get old like me, and they will realise
> what it is like to be laughed at. But I have
> only a few years left now, and I don't care if
> I die tomorrow, I just don't care nomore.

John, 13.

> No money no food
> And only rags to wear
> Nothing to pawn except the ring I wear
>
> Walking down the same old streets
> I have holes in my shoes
> And my coat's split
> My shirt is a piece of cloth to keep
>   me warm.
>
> My harmonica keeps me alive
> I beg for my life
> I can hardly see
> No one talks to a tramp like me.

John, 15.

I was standing at a bus stop with Tony, a fifteen-year old school leaver, and an old, drunken man staggered to us. The bus arrived and we got on, but before the old man got on, the conductor rang the bell and the bus drew away. Tony was very angry and cursed at the conductor. As soon as he got off the bus and came into my flat, he went to my typewriter and typed this:

THE LONE ONE

The old man sways about
as if his life is draining out,
he tries to get a bus,
but the bus goes —
They don't want him he knows.

Just because he's drunk
they think he's a moron,
but he's not, he's human
just like you and me.
They think, 'Don't let him on
he might do a pee.'

The poor old man thinks,
'They don't want me,
well, they're wrong it's
the other way round.
I don't want them,
I would rather be
Poor and happy
than rich and sad.'

Tony Hussey.

For a group of twelve-year old girls writing a play, the 'tramp' became accepted as a younger and more romantic idea, a 'Gipsy Davy' figure who was accepted as something attractive, yet dangerous. But there was still the same strong level of acceptance of a figure who is normally totally rejected:

69

CAST

Kathy   — *a housewife. Full of gossip.*
Polly   — *another housewife. Same as Kathy.*
Jack   — *a tramp. Always roaming about the market.*
Sue   — *family's got a lot of money. Nice kind girl.*
Mother   — *moaning type.*
Father   — *an office man.*

SCENE 1.   IN THE MARKET

KATHY   Do you know that girl Sue who's father works in an
         office? She's been hanging around with that tramp Jack
         lately.
POLLY   You don't say. I bet her mother don't know about it.
         There they are over there.
KATHY   It ain't right, a girl of her standard going about with a
         boy like that.
POLLY   I think it's bad for the image meself. I bet her mother
         and father don't know about it.
SUE   There's a lot of gossip going around about us.
JACK   What can we do about it? Your mother certainly
         wouldn't like me.
SUE   You havn't met me mum yet.
JACK   No I don't think I will.

SCENE 2.   AT SUE'S HOUSE

MOTHER   Hallo Sue, where have you been?
SUE   Nowhere much, only been down the market.
MOTHER   Why don't you find yourself a nice boyfriend?
SUE   Well, I was going to tell you. I've already got a boy.
MOTHER   What's his name, and bring him home to see us.
SUE   His name's Jack and he's not the sort of boy for
         interviews.
MOTHER   I bet he's a nice wealthy boy.
FATHER   Hallo Joan, hallo Sue,— having another mother's
         meeting.

SUE   Just discussing boys.

SCENE 3.   AT THE PARK

JACK   Shall we go for a walk?
SUE   I want to go to the pictures.
JACK   You know I can't afford it.
SUE   Well, I'll pay.
JACK   I'm not the sort of boy who lets girls pay for a night out.
SUE   Well, get a job then.
JACK   You're not leading my life.
SUE   Well, go your own way then.
JACK   Well, see ya.
SUE   See you then.

Sue walks off home.

SCENE 4.   AT HOME

SUE   Mum, I've got something to tell you. *(Starts crying)*.
MUM   What's a matter?
SUE   Mum I'm pregnant.
MUM   You sure?
SUE   Positive, I went for a check up, but the boy who is responsible has left me.
MUM   Have you told him?
SUE   He didn't give me time to.
MUM   Who is he?
SUE   Just a tramp.

Poetry is a respecter of people, and the poetic act is an act of generosity. It is also a great leveller, and when such a homeless and socially rejected man speaks himself of his own plight, he is absolutely on the same living level as those who write about him and move through poetry to share his experiences. The literal truth comes through this man's words; the strength, the stamina:

71

LIFE IN THE SPIKE

They scratched and they scraped
And not enough in their plate
They still strived on
Whipped by the system's thong.
From the fading gloom
They for once (methinks) gleamed the light
And that was only the beginning of one night.

John Crowe

When we showed a poem called *'Shadows of the Night'* by a
sixteen-year old girl to a group of dossers by an open fire in a back
street in Spitalfields, they said they had had a lot of people writing
about them and photographing them: journalists, researchers, social
workers. But they had never read such depth of understanding and
compassion for their situation anywhere before this:

SHADOWS OF THE NIGHT

They are the people of the night
Walking along the streets
Cold, hungry and sometimes drunk.
When people pass by
They circle wide
Not feeling the hurt
The night people feel
Not knowing or caring why
They live like animals
Finding food in dustbins.

They make their homes
On dumps and in fallen down houses,
On door steps or in the roads,
In parks or benches in churches
And even in the house of God.
They are turned out

In to the rain and cold
Of the night.

Finding more shelter
They cover themselves
With newspapers or torn blankets,
For their clothes
No longer keep them warm
For they are old and torn
Like their owners,

Torn apart by people.
Who do not understand
And despise them.
Torn apart by children
Who torment them,
Throwing stones and tins
At them when they pass,
Torn apart by the world.

The rats and other night creatures
Run over their cold stiff bodies
At night.
They bite them and tear
At their flesh,
And sometimes the clothes
Become their shelter.

In the day
They walk along the roads
Stopping people for money.
How many of us humane humans
Walk by nose in the air
Looking at them as if they
were the lowest of the low?

So stop hurting them
And help them.

Moira, 16.

In the launderette, the new village well, people talk to each other and get to know each other. It can become an important focal community point. Here, three eleven-year old boys create such new relationships and a friendship is made in the face of suspicion and bigotry. This is English for empathy:

LAUNDERETTE

SCENE   AT THE LAUNDERETTE

Mrs. Brown and Mrs. Walker talking in the launderette.

MRS. WALKER   What about the new supermarket?
MRS. BROWN   Not bad, but I like the little shops better.
MRS. WALKER   Flo, (Mrs. Brown) your machine stopped.

Mrs. Peters enters, trying to catch her breath.

MRS. PETERS   Thanks a lot Flo. I've been waiting since half
              twelve for you to come round.
MRS. BROWN   Oh Mrs. Peters, I forgot all about it, I knew there
              was something I had forgot.
MRS. WALKER((Sees to her machine). Well, my George as been ill,
              ain't he?
MRS. PETERS   Oh, I didn't know that, did I? Well, I got to go
              now. Wish George better for me.

Tramp enters. Women start to mutter.

MRS. WALKER   I think I'll go with Flo (Mrs. Peters). He smells.
MRS. BROWN   I feel sorry for him. He hasn't got no money and I
              wonder what he wants.
TRAMP   Could you borrow me two bob for the machine?
MRS. WALKER   I wouldn't lend tramps nothing.
MRS. BROWN   What have you got to wash?
TRAMP   Only an old pair of trousers and a shirt.
MRS. BROWN   Well, give em us here and I'll do them for you.

The tramp and Mrs. Brown get on very well and now they are good mates. Every Thursday when Mrs. Brown goes to the laundry, the tramp meets her and she washes his trousers and shirt for him. And Mrs. Walker never talked to Mrs. Brown again because she thinks she has caught fleas from the old tramp.

The empathetic experience may create insights in a child's mind that are well beyond her age. The poem called *'Blindman'* written by an eleven-year old girl who was in the remedial form of the lowest year in her school, and so in the lowliest class of the school, makes the best comment on the absurdity of her educational placement:

BLINDMAN

As I walk along the street
As blind as a bat
I think
I will never see the world
'till I die.

As a blind man
I can't see one thing
In this lovely world
Dark is a terrible thing
To live with.

Leslie, 11.

And Ramona's poem, dramatic and horrific, captures a mind involved in a sensational, but very real social situation:

Loneliness, all these people and no one to share my
    loneliness with
Smiles, false smiles, never a day goes by without a
    false smile.
The worries all seem to come to me.

Why did Sue have to die?
Why did the house catch fire?
Why wasn't I there to save her?
The firemen It was their fault, they didn't get there
    soon enough.
All the people crowded round watching.
Watching them carry out my baby,
My poor burnt baby.
She was only 10, she was too young to die.
Why couldn't it have been me?
The memories haunt me at night.
If I wasn't so selfish, I'd have stayed home with her
And missed Bingo for once.

And imagining one of the most harrowing and terrifying of
experiences, a fifteen year-old girl realised how the violently unequal
economic and class structure of British society forces some people
to undergo terrible ordeals:

I've been through the pain before
We could find the money
I don't want to kill it,
it's human like me.
What shall I do?
I will have to find the money
To have the
    ABORTION
The money I pay to have
    it done would be able
    to pay for my
    CHILD
    if I let it live
    which I don't think
    I will
I have four other kids
Why can't I make it five?
We'll manage somehow . . .

While I was thinking this
The abortion has been
Done.
Now it's all over . . .

Janice, 15.

Animals are also neighbours, neighbours who can soften a hard brick city. But they can also be far more. A child may say things about an animal or bird which she may, because of reticence, never say about people. A lot of love and attention will be given to animals by children, and very often that animal becomes personified in terms which express great compassion:

THE OLD BIRD

The old Bird has Broken wings.
The old Bird can Hardly sing
The old Bird can only stare
The old Bird can not Bear
The Hot weather nor the cold.

What sort of Bird is the old Bird.
What sort of things can it do.
What sort of things can He say
Can He fly, can He cry,
I sometimes wonder this as I walk By.

Kim, 11.

Sometimes it is as if the child identifies with the animal to such an extent that the mind becomes the object it rests upon. Marion, looking at a pigeon in the sky, flies up with it, and seems to escape into the clouds:

DISAPPEARANCE

I saw a pigeon
flying across the sky
it was black and white
it seemed like an aircraft flying high
it flew up and down, round and round
saw some other birds it did
I think it was scared
it flew like an eagle
flew right to the sun
then it disappeared in the clouds.

Marion, 11.

A child's admission of love and friendship is very open with animals, and the fear of being rejected or ridiculed does not occur: the animal gives and accepts love. And the first experience of the realities of birth and death may be through animals. For the child, this may be absolutely real:

THE DAY OUR DOG DIED

It was Sunday morning when I awoke
To see the face of my mum.
She, her eyes full of tears, said
Softly, unsteadily, 'She . . . She's
Gone in her sleep.'
I felt upset, yet in a way
Happy —
For she was blind and almost deaf
But full of life.
It seemed a cruel kind of thing,
Like one of the family had died.
I waited until my mum had gone,
And for a while cried.
I went downstairs, my head aching
And my dog gone.

Ramona, 11.

It is as if anything that exists can have life for the poet. There are very few trees in Spitalfields. Tony saw one, dying, decaying, and wrote this:

The poor tree whithers
It whithers and dies
no one cares they just
walk by
Once it was a lovelie
tree so high it almost
reach the sky,
just like any thing else
It dies
poor tree.

Empathy stretches anywhere, parents, friends, tramps, neighbours, animals, trees, It reaches into things, objects, which have no life and fills them with living. Ramona's extraordinary poem, *'The Stall and Me'*, is a consummate achievement. She saw a Ron McCormick photograph of a doll on a jumble stall in a market, and her mind she became the doll. For her, the act of poetry has set in motion imaginative energy at its most compassionate and generous. She tells the story with a grasp of character and narrative skill that expands her eleven years into a lifetime. Her poem is a huge act of social love:

THE STALL AND ME

'Earrings for sale, 'nuckle dusters, watch straps,'
The man who owns the stall cries,
'Second-hand beads.'
He stops talking as a lorry rushes past and drowns his voice,
The exhaust choked his words into a cough
Lorry after lorry
Car after car.
I sit here waiting patiently
Waiting for someone to buy me
For someone to take me home and love me.

Once again the man resume his voice and yells,
'Cowboy suits, buttons, buckles,'
An old age pensioner wanders to the stall
Clutching a one pound note.
The owner got up off the old orange box that his backside
lazily rested upon,
The old lady's small grey eyes wandered over my body . . .
The owner grabbed me and said
'This 'ere doll's a real bargin,
Only two pounds ten.'
The woman said, 'I've only a pound, and it's my grand-
    daughter's birthday tomorrow.'
She explained how this was all she had left.
The owner said, 'I'm sorry luv, I don't give fings away,
What about these beads?'
But the lady insisted that she wanted me.
The owner, being a kindly man, said,
'Go 'ome and bring me another ten bob.'
A small tear fell from my eyes
As the old lady slumped off.
The owner knew he would never see the old lady again . . .
Dolls have feelings too you know!
The owner of the stall
Ran after her thrusting me into her hand.
The next day her grandchild pushed me past the stall,
The owner was still crying out.
He waved and smiled —
Perhaps he'll be there for ever
But he'll always be just the stall owner.
I'll never know his name
And I'll never forget his dirty little stall in Petticoat Lane.

Ramona, 11.

Some neighbours may be newer than others, and sometimes they may have different languages, different coloured skins, different cultures. A thirteen-year old North London boy speaks of his own street:

My street is named Sellons Ave.
It is a quiet road.
Different people live in it.
Pakistanis, Coloured, and Foreign people.
We're all good friends.
We play a lot of football.
Our Mums talk a lot to each other
We usually sit and play records
in each other's houses.
We borrow a lot, sugar, tea etc.
I have lived in Sellons for all
My life, so far.
So have most of the other boys.

Thomas O'Connell, 13.

It is this willingness to communicate and co-operate which builds up a whole sense of a working community, a collective community where the divisions between people have been crushed, and where individual, racial and ethnic identities are upheld with a wider community which serves a united, multi-racial working class. George Jackson wrote, a few days before his death: 'Without the collective sense of community, without its movement and institutions, we simply never will be an effective force.'

The school is such an 'institution' that should serve the community and cut itself off from outside manipulation. A priority of its education experiences should be the breaking of racism and differences amongst ourselves caused by those people from outside trying to run our lives. The cementation of a unified working class community has to be the achievement of those people living and participating within it. The schools must pursue and implement this struggle to create a strong, unified community with a secure, unashamed identity. The English teacher works towards this idea through the skills of the written and spoken word, and the love and empathy of the powers of the imagination. Although for our self-respect we must accept and affirm our race, black or white, it is imperative that we more strongly and committedly affirm our class loyalties together, black and white workers. It is the strongest social factor that unites us.

The differences between races are normally created by outside social pressures forced upon the working class: unemployment, bad housing, low wages, failure and impotence of the 'race relations industry', and historical bigotries and dominations. It becomes the responsibility of members of the community to take these problems into their own hands and deal with them themselves, creating their own multi-racial infrastructure. We cannot trust the external, exploiting people who are organised to keep us apart. The teacher-neighbour has a particular responsibility to spread communication in this context. He is a 'word conductor', he must spread the words and images which stimulate and strengthen identity and harmony.

Initially, the problem of racial disunity can only be tackled by communication, by taking stock of the reasons and insecurities behind the hostility, and by trying to articulate them. Just after the East Pakistan cyclone disaster in 1970, some thirteen-year old girls wrote these comments. The cyclone was only seen as a pretext for them to put down their anger and resentment towards Pakistani immigrant neighbours:

THE DISASTER

So what, so what of the disaster,
It's nothing to do with us,
Why tell us about it?
Why make all the fuss?

There's other countries in the world,
Not only England you know,
They shouldn't have let them over here,
For now it's time to go.

They are dirty, they smell, and they live in
    disgrace,
You can tell what they are like, by the
    look on their face,
Other countries won't have them,
So they bung them on with us,
But why should we take care of them?
Why should we make all the fuss?

I can't understand when people say,
"They can't help it if their made that way!"
Of course they can't help it,
I understand that,
But why come over here?
What about Paki-Land?
I'm sure they can't be proud of that!

'IT'S US AGAIN'

I like the way the papers say
ah! what a shame to them,
never our kids get the chance
to feel the hurt
or pain.
Because one day those Pakis say
we'll have your house your
home,

then all them men in papers say
why don't we send them home.
I think all the government must
be mad cause we arnt the
only ones,
It's us whites that get the blame
if ever the tide comes.
I love the people that seem to
say God bless the poor soul
but if ever they move next
door,
you want to send them home

Before you give your opinion
I must stop and say.
Would they ever do the same
to us as we are helping they?

PAKISTAN

Myself am a person following Enoch Powell.
In the area where I live they are 10 to every
1 of us. They smell and are dirty, they breed
like flies. They don't know how to behave.
They have got slimy looks about them. They
only come over here and go straight on the
National Assistance. When my dad was in
hospital, my mum went to this place and I was
with her, we saw a paki get at least £5.20.
My mum was very angry. He had a wife and 4
or 5 kids. My mum, alright she only had 3
kids but she got half as much as he got.
My opinion is send them all back or line them
up an shoot the lot of them, *dead*.
Where I live about 3 or 4 years ago we had a
complete Jewish market, now it is completely
Pakis, you might find 1 or 2 Jewish shops.
They annoy me when they give you their usual
slimy looks and whistle.

Answer one question:- Why do we let them into
England when Australia don't.

The indignation behind the words is mostly socially caused:
suspicion of a strange, unusual culture, defensiveness of national
identity, fear of being over-run, resentment towards foreign people
benefiting from what seems to be the hard-pressed welfare state,
and the rhetoric of racist politicians. The statements suggest an
armed camp already being formed and mobilised. The reason for the
hostility however, is not all economic, or rational, or based on social
causation. Much of the aggression is unthinking, overtly and distinctly
emotionally caused: the hostility to the Asian smells, the 'slimy
looks', the 'disgrace' of their habits. The racial barrier, formed
emotively by a succession of animal impulses and suspicions,
broadens and engulfs rational thought. It moves viciously towards
sadism:

> I walked along Brick Lane
> On a Sunday afternoon
> Where I saw a Pakistani
> Eating curry with a spoon.
>
> Later that day I walked by again
> Only to see the Paki in pain
> He was lying helplessly on the ground
> With bottles and blood all around.
>
> The Pakistanis they do smell
> I think that they should go to Hell
> There is ground in dirt in their knees
> And in their hair they do have fleas.

Boy, 13.

The emotional, irrational block makes the factual truth of the real
economic situation and class basis difficult to communicate. Instead
of learning with a socially conscious mind the facts and information

about the life-habits and culture of the immigrant group and joining together in a mutual struggle against common exploiters, a humorous defence is built. This defence cannot work with fact, or truth, it only works with exaggeration and fantasy. Any neutral or objective area of the mind, which would impartially accept fact or information is lost. Instead of a precise documentation or expression of the problem, the irrational, racist bias creates ridiculous overstatements. In the wake of Powell's 'rivers of blood' we have:

CYCLONE

Thousands of pakis killed by the wind
Thousands killed by the water
Thousands of pakis killed by disease
Thousands killed by starvation
and millions come over here.
Thousands of pakis killed by skinheads
Thousands killed by the grease
and none of them never go home.

Boy, 15.

It is this exaggerating element which creates the racist joke, always based on the fantasy vision of the victimised group, who are hopelessly caricatured to create more irrational impulses: laughter and ridicule. A class of white fourth form school leavers used an opportunity to write about the Pakistanis in the East End, in these terms:

ADVENTURE

We was on safari in a densely populated area. Then a pakistani come running past and then he was eaten by a huge rat and all that was left of him was his mohair turban. So we took a couple of trophies of rats heads and went home. Believe it or not this was in HESSEL Street.

We stood on a corner waiting for a pak to come along
then we herd a pak wisterling the pak nashonal antonon
(riding along on the crest of a wave) we wated till he
passed us then we gave him a good boot up the Kiber
pass he screamed and then fell 'That boot must have
made contact with his nuts' said Sam, look he's spewing
Kitty Kat you must have really kicked him hard. Then
he rolled on to his side and we started frisking him
for doe but all I found in his wallet was a picture
of his 9 wives and 62 kids. Then in the carrier
bags I saw 72 portions of curry. Then he vometted
and died.

The boat landed at Gangi delta 100 paks got aboard
the boat and then it salled out to sea. The caption
told them to wear lead boots to stop the noise (the
mugs put them on) then suddenly a terrible scream
came from below a pak had his nuts in a thumb screw
for drinking a pint of curry then the caption said
he was going for a midnight row and then suddenly
the boat sank with 100 paks with lead boots and
one with crushed nuts. And the only evidence was
100 turbins floating on the water.

One way to combat this situation is to spread communication and
information about the victimised group, to compensate for the lack
of knowledge about that group of the 'host' culture, to emphasise
that this is the working class dividing and victimising itself. This
means an 'education' of the 'host' group out of its antipathy to the
new immigrant culture by giving such knowledge and facts as would
hopefully break down the ignorance barriers. But a violence and
hostility that is irrationally conceived often needs also to be
irrationally resolved and broken. One answer seemed to be to engage
the sympathy and empathy of poetry and drama: to try to set into
motion sympathetic and generous impulses and emotions through
the imagination. I used a number of Don McCullin photographs of
the people of East Pakistan after the 1970 cyclone, and Ron
McCormick's photographs of the Pakistanis of Spitalfields and

Whitechapel to stimulate some kind of emotional and creative response. At first, the effect seemed to cause a confirmation of the stand the boys were taking. One boy wrote this poem when he saw a photograph of a staring Bengali boy with an empty plate. I had suggested that he might imagine the thoughts of the boy while the photograph was being taken:

> I am hungry I'm starving
> I need some curry 'gallons'
> 'please' let me go on national assistance .
> You with the camera take me back
> to England, and brick lane or essel st
> the paradise of pakis

Another boy was similarly unsympathetic when the situation was changed to London:

> We sat in the flat Me My wife My ten children
> My brother Ali and his wife and our mother and
> father and all there brothers and sisters and our
> aunts and uncles we were tucking into our Kitty
> Kat and curry when suddenly the door was smashed
> down and in came 40 skinheads 39 fainted with the
> smell and one caught cholera and died instantilly
> and that was one victory for us

The joke continued for them. But other boys seemed to create more generous attitudes through their poetry, their words were becoming the poetry of solidarity:

> I am in Pakistan,
> Cold and hungary filled with fear,
> most of my relatives are in the pile,
> the pile that are nothing but DEAD,

The pile of dead are all there,
all now bloated, but not with fear,
the fear has been washed out,
all because of the cyclone that hit our land

I am only one of the few,
one of the people that missed the queue,
I might die very soon,
and it's all because of that great cyclone.

The issue soon shifted from Bengal to problems and insecurities at home. A group of twelve year-old boys began to see that one of the activities most important in their lives was also a huge social leveller:

SCENE   THE FOOTBALL TEAM GETTING CHANGED

MICKY   Old Roberts is bringing that pakky kid for a trial today. Wonder what his name is.
DANNY   Look, here comes Roberts, and he's got that pakky.

The boys run to the window.

GINO   He looks tough to me.
KEITH   Watch out Gino, he'll stab you with the knife he's got tucked up his shorts.

They enter the room.

ROBERTS   This is the new boy, his name is Kermat.
KERMAT   HALLO everybody.

There is a pause of silence, then

EVERYBODY   HALLO there kermat.
MICKY   I don't want no pakky in this football team. I might leave if Roberts says so.

GINO	Yeah, so will I.
KEITH	He might not be good enough to play for the school team.
DANNY	Let's go outside and play. We'll show him up.
NARRATER	They go outside, the boys do their best they can to show him up, but he shows them up.

The fourth form class also began to deal with their unwelcome neighbours in the surroundings of their own streets. One fifteen year-old boy wrote down a very strong reminiscence:

> I can remember when we did go Paki-bashing. There was
> three of us, John, Micky and myself, and John had an
> iron cube. We asked the Paki the time. He lifted
> his arm and told us, and when he went on the iron thing
> struck him on the back. He ran, and we chased him into
> the mission down Stepney Way near New Road. We waited,
> then six to eight Pakis came out of the mission with
> lumps of wood. We run and came out behind the London
> Hospital where there were a few crates of bottles
> left there for the milkman. Micky stopped me, and
> John ran on a little way and Micky stood there
> throwing bottles at the Pakis. Me and John told
> him to hurry up. He came and the Pakis chased us a
> little way and then gave up and the three of us killed
> ourselves laughing. But it was not funny at the time.

I read his account, and was very impressed by the honesty and detail it expressed. I asked him about the man who was struck. Did he know him? 'No.' What do you think his feelings were when he was jumped on? 'I don't know, really'. I said that he'd written this from his own mind, his own situation, now why didn't he write and try to imagine the incident from the mind and experience of the man who had been struck? Why not become this man for five minutes and try to say what he felt and thought during those moments? Ten minutes later the boy had written this:

It was not all that late when I was walking home, but it was dark. And at the bottom of the street there were a bunch of the so-called skinheads by my shop. And I could feel myself trembling. I saw one of the boys pick up a brick. He brought his arm back and threw the brick through my window. I ran towards them shouting, thinking that they would get scared and run, but they just stood there as if they were waiting for me. I was not more than ten yards away when I stopped. They came at me joking about what they were going to do. Then one walked behind me. I followed him with my eyes. Then they jumped me, took the money what I had to keep my family with. They beat me up real bad and I could feel the blood running down my face. I could just not understand it, and I just sat on the pavement crying and thinking . . . Why? It's not because they don't like us, and bloody Hell man, what makes them think we love them?

For me, this was a victory for the power of the imagination and the power of words. Such expression, and the sentiments generated by that expression, can never be just a transient, ephemeral state. Once you have climbed inside the mind of another person, you can never completely escape. You have shared his thoughts, his emotions, his world, and it has become a part of you and your world. You have extended yourself beyond yourself, and you are larger. You have built a bridge, as this boy had done. He mobilised his generosity in a direction which had been blocked before. His seriousness seemed to have an effect. The same group of boys who had caricatured, exaggerated and laughed at the problem before, suddenly became very earnest when they worked together to write a short play about experiences they knew too well:

PAKI-BASHING

SCENE   *East End of London just off Commercial Rd. where Paki-Bashing was started.*

1ST BOY	Fancy beating up a gunga?
2ND BOY	Don't mind.
1ST BOY	Where abouts can we do it?
2ND BOY	Just around the corner. You know er Hessel St.
1ST BOY	Come on then.

They leave the corner and start off for Hessel St. No Paks.

1ST BOY	None here, come on we'll walk down there, there must be some down there. You can smell em from here.
2ND BOY	There's one, come on.
1ST BOY	Hang on, you gona do it?
2ND BOY	I'll go round here, you go and ask him the time.
1ST BOY	Who gonna whack him first?
2ND BOY	I'll jump on his back, and you kick him in the nuts.
1ST BOY	Alright, but don't let me down. Oh if he pulls a blade don't run into him.
2ND BOY	He won't, they just stand there and shit themselves.
1ST BOY	Got the time mate?

He raises his arm to look at his watch. Second boy jumps him.

PAK	OH NO
1ST BOY	Come on fuck your
PAK	Murder ooh!
2ND BOY	That's him done. Watch it his got a knife.
1ST BOY	Get him, come on, AHH his caught me.
2ND BOY	Quick here comes his mates.
1ST BOY	Cut out quick.

They run from the Pak and throw bottles.
Away from the scene.

1ST BOY	That was close, I'm really sweating.
2ND BOY	Must have cut him, your full of blood.
1ST BOY	Must have punched me in the gut, I can feel a pain.
2ND BOY	See if it's bruised or anything.
1ST BOY	Here, I'm bleeding, Oh God he must have stabbed me.
2ND BOY	Come on, we'll go up the hospital.
1ST BOY	Fuck off, when they find out about the Pak there know it's me.

2ND BOY	Spouse so.
1ST BOY	I don't feel to good, you know. I feel right bad.
2ND BOY	What you gonna tell you old girl? Fred, don't muck about.

Fred's on the floor.

1ST BOY	My legs gave away, oh its only a scratch. Let's go.
2ND BOY	Close tonight, he could have done you.
1ST BOY	I feel sorry for him in a way.
2ND BOY	I suppose so.
1ST BOY	I don't mind West Indians but I hate the Gungas.
1ST BOY	He's still human isnt he?
2ND BOY	He is a bit I sapouse.
1ST BOY	You know what I mean.
2ND BOY	Well what are you gonna tell your old girl?
1ST BOY	I'll tell her I had a knuckle with some geezer.
2ND BOY	Yeah that should do the trick.

On the way home.

2ND BOY	Well, are you gonna go after him later, perhaps next week or something?
1ST BOY	No, it really was my fault. I mean, you can't really blame him, can you?
2ND BOY	Yeah but
1ST BOY	But nothing, he done me, fair.
2ND BOY	Yeah well I see you tomorrow night.
1ST BOY	Yeah but, you know like, no gunga hunting.
2ND BOY	All right, I spouse thats the best thing because you could have had it tonight. See ya.
1ST BOY	See ya.

THE END

This is a play about rough justice, street justice, but through it, the co-authors have come to a situation where they have acquired a kind of respect for people whom they had previously dismissed and vilified. They all left school as soon as they could, at the end of the

Easter or Summer terms, and this was one of the last pieces of writing they did in their English lessons. Through their imaginations they had constructed a play, extended their sympathies and respect — 'He's still human isn't he', was for them, a massive admission — and committed themselves, through imaginative experience, to the acceptance of new attitudes. And they had generated these attitudes themselves, through their own dramatic experience. It may have been very little, but it may have been a lot.

For the fourth form East End girl who wrote this next story, the transportation of herself inside a victimised neighbour has been voluntary, wholehearted and complete:

My name's Adion Musacan. I have come from Pakistan.
I have been in England for one month. I've heard
that the young white boys have been going round
beating my countrymen up.

I have never had such an experience like this, until
one dark November night. It was a Sunday night. I
had been to a meeting of my Pakistan fellow countrymen.
We were discussing the problem of these white boys
beating us up. We were told to go around in groups.
The meeting ended at eight o'clock. I was going to walk
along with Ali, Mocas, and Johnas. I didn't really know
them but it was someone to walk along with. I wanted to
go to the toilets so I asked them to wait for me. I
could not find the toilets. I must have been a very
long while, because when I came out to the front they
were gone.

I felt a funny sensation in my stomach. I was very
frightened. I had to go from Commercial Road to Aldgate
East. I was going to get a bus, but I would have to wait
and this was very risky. You have a better chance if
you are walking. If I stay to the main road I may have
a chance. I walked hurriedly along the road hoping to
meet with some of my Pakistan friends. I neared the
split of Commercial Road on to Mile End Road. I was
nearly home. I crossed Mile End Road. Not one skinhead

95

had I seen. All I had to do now was to go down Club Row.
Then in the light of the lamp-post I see about four
figures walking towards me. My heart was beating fast.
I turned to go the other way and there were more figures.
The figures were well spread over the length of the street.
'It's a little Pak.'
I did not say nothing. The figures were taking form, . . .
the boots, the sheepskins, the big black coats. I did not
know what to do. A voice shouted 'Get him lads.' They
ran toward me. I heard the thumping of their feet. I
was dumb struck. I couldn't move or shout for help. I
felt the first boot. I did not fall or cry out. Something
inside me stopped me from screaming as the hard boots were
digging in my head and body. Why should I cry out? It
would give them the greatest of pleasure to hear me screaming.
No I will not scream.

I curled up in a little ball. The kicks were getting more
painful.
'This one thinks he's a really hard case.'
'He's took a lot of stick and he ain't screaming.'
'I'll make him scream.'
A piercing boot kicked me in my side. I was feeling very
weak. Could I hold on, soon they would go. I must not cry
out. I will show them I am not scared of them. I did not
know where my new born courage had come from. The kicks
were getting fainter.
'Come on let's go. He ain't going to cry.'
The feet slowly walked away.
'I enjoy that. I like a good kick in now and again.'
'Yeah it was good.'
All of a sudden everything went black. The next thing I knew I
was in hospital.

Lorraine, 15.

Another fourth form boy in the same class as the writers of 'Paki-
Bashing' completely overcame the divisions of race, age, continents
and life-experience. He was a fifteen year-old white Londoner,

becoming through his poetry a Bengali man working in London for his family trapped in an Asian catastrophe, trying to make sense of tragedy:

A PAKISTANI MAN THINKING ABOUT THE FLOOD

They kick us,
They boot us to the ground
For no reason,
They call us names,
They make jokes about us.
We live in a house that's derelict
But we are grateful,
For it is better than nothing.
They cannot feel the pain,
But what has happened in Pakistan
And to my parents —
For I know not what has happened
To them —
The tidal wave
It came so quick
They were terrified in their tracks,
Helpless,
My wife, my children
Dead,
Thousands dead and drowned.
Why?

Peter, 15.

Charlie Mason, a twelve year-old white boy, had very strong feelings about the plight of Pakistanis in the East End, particularly the children trapped in a white, hostile group. His poem is testimony to the ultimate criterion of poetry: its generousness:

I am just a pakystani Boy
No one likes me

When I think of all the boys playing
I wish they would let me play
But no, they put their fingers over their noses
And say go away.
I wish that I wasn't born
I wish I was in pakystan choping corn
It would be great
I would play till very late

In the 'Paki-Bashing' play, one of the boys says, 'I don't mind West Indians, but I hate the Gungas.' In Stepney, West Indians often tend to be isolated inside the white community rather than have any other collective sense of community with other black people. The cultural barriers hardly exist: the white youth in fact, admire and imitate many aspects of the English West Indian's lifestyle, such as his music or his clothes sense. Economically, black and white have few differences, very few people have a great deal of money. The only barrier that remains is the final one, the barrier that is ultimately erected despite the strongest elements of mutual acceptance, and similarity of social situation: race, colour. In the first of the following two passages, a white fourth form girl talks about a black friend from her own impression of her friend. In the second passage she becomes the other girl herself:

I have a few black friends, but they always make me
feel as though I am just using them to fill up any
spare time I have. If I go and call for Sally, she
only comes out if there is a group of us going somewhere, she is like this with us all. I think that
she is afraid to go out with one of us alone because
she feels that she won't be able to talk about anything other than records. She doesn't go out with
boys because she is afraid of them. She is all right
if she is just talking to a boy, but if she likes the
boy, she is shy. She might be shy because she
goes to an all-girls' school.

My name is Sally, and I am a Jamaican girl. I
only have a few black friends but they live a long
way away and they can't come down all the time.
I really enjoy myself when I go to visit them.
They always seem to have a lot to do. There is a
black family with a girl about my age just moved in
the new flats across the road. Perhaps I will make
friends with her in time. When I am with my white
friends, I can't think of anything to say to them
because we have hardly anything in common, except
school and they like the kind of records I like.
I don't like talking to them on their own because
after about five minutes I can't think of anything
else to say, and it is left up to them to do all the
talking and I feel awkward. It is best when they come
to call for me in a group because then they are all
talking and I don't feel as left out as usual.

It is this view of race as a barrier that polarises relationships around separate colours, and disallows their development and fruition. It is a view which isolates people, cuts them off from each other. The easiest, most instinctive and natural thing to do, it seems, is to fall back to one's own group and succumb to the easy security that may exist there. This is not a natural response. It is a conditioned response, conditioned by social, racist and often family pressures that speak out in fear and insecurity against discovery, new relationships, new identities. In this play, the five fifteen year-old girls present their conclusions about an oppressed, stifled relationship which never had the chance to grow:

LOVE RELATIONSHIP

ACTORS:
Barry — coloured boy
Carol — coloured boy's girlfriend
Mother — Florry
Father — Bill
Carol's brother, Ricky

AT THE HOUSE

MUM	Carol where are you going tonight?
CAROL	No-where special.
MUM	That's what you always say, if you've got a boyfriend, you know that you're dad and me don't mind you having boyfriends, because you had one or two before, have you got a boyfriend now?
CAROL	No, no, I haven't got a boyfriend why don't you leave me alone, nag, nag, nag, that's all I get from you and I'm fed up with it.
MUM	I only asked dear.
CAROL	I'm sorry mum, I didn't mean it, I don't know what came over me. I'm going now see you later be home by half eleven, ta ta.
MUM & DAD	Bye, bye, dear don't be late.

AT THE CAFE BARRY IS WAITING

BARRY	You're late.
CAROL	Yeah I know, I had a bit of a row with me mum.
BARRY	About me? or don't she know yet.
CAROL	She don't know yet but I've got to tell her soon. Other wise she will hear the gossip and it will be worse for us.
BARRY	Come lets go to the pictures now or we will be late.
CAROL	Alright.

Out side the pictures is Carol's brother, Ricky and his mates hanging about.

RICKY	Carol.
CAROL	Hello Ricky,
BARRY	Who's that.
CAROL	My brother Ricky.
BARRY	Oh.
RICKY	Who's he.
CAROL	My boyfriend.
RICKY	You mean you go out with a black boy.
CAROL	Yea whats the matter with that the trouble with you is that your the best friend of Enock Powell I thought seeing as your my brother you would understand.
RICKY	Don't give that rubbish does mum know.
CAROL	No I aint told her yet.
RICKY	Well you better tell her before I do.
CAROL	You mean you would tell her.
RICKY	Yeah I don't want my sister to go with a black boy.
CAROL	You make me sick you know that. Come on Barry.
BARRY	Your brothers right you know you will get a bad name.
CAROL	Whats a matter with you, having second thoughts. Look I don't care what people say or think as long as we like each other it don't matter.
BARRY	Look lets go home to your mum now, come on I'm there so don't worried.
CAROL	No Barry, lets go tomorrow and I'll break it to her easy.
BARRY	What do you mean break the news cos I'm black you say it as I've got the plague.

101

Carol arrives home to find her mother making tea in the kitchen.

CAROL   Hello, mum.
MUM   Hello, had a nice time.
CAROL   Yeah, it was alright.

(There's a pause while Carol try's to say it)

CAROL   Mum I've got a boyfriend.
MUM   I thought so. See I didn't bite your head off, Whats his name.
CAROL   Barry. Can I bring him up tomorrow night.
MUM   Me and your father are going for a drink so we can only see him for a few minutes.
CAROL   That's alright we'll stay in and watch telly, is that alright.
MUM   Of course dear I don't mind, he sounds a nice boy.
RICKY   Hello mum, hello Carol, wheres dad?
MUM   He's gone to the pub, he'll be back soon. Did you know Carol had a boyfriend.
RICKY   So she told you, so you don't mind him being black.

Everything goes silent.

MUM   Carol you didn't tell me he was, well coloured did you.
CAROL   Does it make that much difference.
MUM   Of course it does.
CAROL   Why? Come on tell me, why nag at me because I haven't got a boyfriend then you nag when I have.
MUM   But he's coloured.
CAROL   So your another friend of Enoch Powell.
MUM   Don't be silly.
CAROL   What do you mean don't be silly it's you thats being silly the trouble with you is your colour prejudice.
RICKY   Wait till your father hears about this.
CAROL   I don't care what any one thinks anymore.
                    Mum if you want me to finish it with him I will.

MUM	No I don't want you to do that because you will only go with him behind my back look why not still bring him back and let me judge for my-self.
CAROL	Thanks mum.

The next night Carol meets Barry and tells him.

CAROL	My mum wants to see you Barry will you come.
BARRY	I don't think I will Carol.
CAROL	Why not.
BARRY	Because well, say if your mum say's it's alright for us to see each other well, and we get serious I don't see you mother and father letting us get married can you? Tell the truth.
CAROL	No but.
BARRY	No buts, lets just part now and be good friends before we get serious but remember I think of you a lot.
CAROL	If you think it will be for the best alright but I will always think of you and it's better to finish it before we get to serious your right Barry well it's been fun.
BARRY	Let me walk you home.
CAROL	Yeah ok.

(Out side Carol's house.)

BARRY	Yeah well give us a kiss and I'll see you around.

(They kissed and Carol goes inside and calls her mum and tells her what happened.)

CAROL	Mum I've finished with Barry.
MUM	Why I told you to bring him home.
CAROL	I know but well it's for the best lets just forget it ok mum.
MUM	Alright love if you want to I won't say anymore now do you want a cup of tea and a sandwich.
CAROL	Yes please mum, what's on television I think it's that comedy show.

THE END

We have to break the conditioning that makes young people so cynical and accepting about what seems to be the inevitable failure of Carol and Barry's relationship. Such relationships need not fail; they are conditioned to fail. We have to look for the points of unity and connection in ourselves, all workers, for our common identity, mutual generosity, and mutual will to oppose an enemy that is using us both and keeping us divided from each other. We are all neighbours, but we must be comrades and lovers also. For our children now, black, brown and white, this search and its success will be heroic. One of the girls who wrote 'Love Relationship' wrote this a week later. She had overcome, as we all must:

BLACK AND WHITE

I'm white, he's black —
is it so bad?
Or is it what people say?
They can say some
nasty things
I know
I've heard them.
Why can't they leave us alone?
It's our lives, we'll do what we want.
But if he was white,
well . . .
that would be different,
'He's one of us,
not them.'
Why can't they just
try
and see it our way?
We can't help it,
It's not that bad,
It's not his fault
he's black
Nor is it our fault
we're white.

Janice, 15.

THE LONG AND WINDING ROAD

In a highly exploitative, competitive society like the British society, the experience of adolescence is both a struggle and a long and winding road. It is the period when the examination system strikes with its greatest intensity, where the truths of aggression, violence and competition in established society are made clear and unequivocal to the child. He is conditioned to believe that success in competition and an aggressive assertion of his own intelligence above those of his fellows will win him his rewards and make him strong: pass your exams, and all is well, because there will always be those who fail. And for those who fail, there is the sudden blow of the dead-end job or the dole queue.

Any real educational experience involves a struggle against this consumptive and destructive syndrome, and the creation of an alternative identity to the exploitative, competitive pattern. The growth of adolescent identity in a particular neighbourhood must involve the construction of a collective co-operative identity that can only grow from a collective imagery, a foundation of mutual language and symbol, which people need to both share experience and achieve a common level of communication.* The images of identity may come across to the child not only through speech — through the neighbourhood imagery of dialect, local phraseology and slang, the place names and local mythology — but also the images of the wider world experienced through the new media: television, radio, cinema and phonograph record. In the two adolescent poems which follow, the impact of the genre of the 'horror' film of television and cinema, is obvious:

* See The Forsaken Lover, (*Penguin, 1973*) for the author's ideas on Language and Identity.

One cold and stormy night
As the moon was full and bright,
What was known as Dracula's power
Came on the stroke of the twelfth hour.

He rose from a coffin from a sleep
While the church bell rang with a creep,
He lives on blood alone
Is always breaking people's bones,
He strikes as the wind upon the branches moans.

As evening falls and morning comes,
He walks away from the London slums.

Margaret, 12.

JACK THE RIPPER

I lurk in the doorways of Whitechapel
In the mists
And the narrow roads
With my knife that is as sharp
As knife through butter.
I hide in the doorways
And slit the whores' throats
Without them making a sound,
And the police are fools
They do not know that I am
    one of them,
But who would look for a killer
So terrifying
Dressed in the Policeman's uniform?
Only me . . .
For I am Jack the Ripper

Peter, 15.

Here, the stark realism of a decaying local environment also becomes the grisly setting of the Hammer horror film, and the images are adopted by the children for their own world.

Adolescence can provoke an internal war, a war of conflicts fought by the emerging identity, to assert itself against a social system that would tame and exploit it. Consequently, the activity of war and violence has a continuous fascination for the adolescent mind trapped in its own insecurity. This generation of young teachers and pupils has not directly experienced war. It has not fought on the battlefields of Europe and North Africa. Yet the new media surround it and bombard it with the images of war. There is real war every night on the six o'clock news, or every morning at the breakfast table: Vietnam, Ulster, Bangladesh. There is the romanticising and exploitation of war and violence that was only ever seen by most men as a cruel necessity. War becomes a gruesome, violent fantasy, leaving its images upon the emerging identity of the child, and giving pounds and dollars to those who make the fantasies. There is also the entire, real thing. I have, tonight just watched a television programme about the Atomic arms race. At one point, it showed a young American woman and a square-jawed American soldier leading a group of uniformed young boys around the Atomic Bomb museum of Albuquerque, New Mexico. The boys were being shown the sights of an Atomic age, and the history and development of Nuclear warfare. One boy, looking at a sign which said 1,000 megatons, said 'What does megaton mean?' 'It means that the bomb has the strength of a thousand million tons of T.N.T.' said the young woman. The soldier added to the commentator, 'What the boy realises is that we need this bomb as a deterrent against the Russians. The war of the adolescent is a real war. Accepting the life-situation today involves the acceptance of a life-situation of total insecurity before the reality of the Atomic age:

> As I sit there thinking
> I hear a strange noise
> I wonder what it is
> So I look out to see what it is
> I can see something
> Dropping from a black cloud.
> Suddenly it falls
> There is thick black smoke

Coming from everywhere
Is it another war?
I just don't know.

Timmy, 11.

ATOMIC AGE

Now there is silent eternity
Godless race wandering across the black universe
Extinguished
Extinguished from the intelligent flame of life
The dark burnt sunless globe
Remains fatherless
Sunless.

Intiaz, 14.

It was seven o'clock, my boy friend and I were at the pictures. Then right in the middle of the film an announcement was made. "Please listen, this announcement is a matter of life and death. Please don't panic. The Russians are going to send nuclear rockets to blow up London. Another announcer will come on after me and tell you where in this district are the nearest emergency shelters. Please don't panic. Go to Green Street Station and they will tell you where to go." Panic was captured in the cinema. People were running and crying, and some were screaming. My boy friend and I decided to sit and wait for the crowd to go, as most of them were hysterical. What-ever happened I was to stay with Mick, my boyfriend. I was frightened, the fear inside nearly sent me mad. The crowds were nearly gone now. Mick told me not to panic, he was good in emergencies. I began to cry "Mick, what about our families." "There be alright, there be alright." He tried to comfort me but it was no good. "The whole of London, Mick, our homes maybe our families, I can't stand it Mick." People were rushing in the direction of the station. Mothers with their children, screaming, hysterical people. My fear was too strong, I was going to die.

Mick was talking to me but I couldn't hear him. There was a block between us. I started screaming, Mick slapped me round the face. "Lorraine we'll be alright don't cry." "I don't want to die, or you to die." At that moment I looked in to his eyes. I love him and I never felt like this before. "Mick stay with me what ever happens, I love you. If we die we will die together." "I will Lorraine I will." We hurried along with the crowds to Green Street Station. There were millions of people crying, screaming and panicking. We tried to get down stairs but they would not let us down. "Go to the city centre." We would never make it in time. There was five minutes to go. I knew I was going to die. But there was no fear now. Yes. "We won't make it, let's go and see if our families are alright." "OK, Lorraine are you frightened?" "No Mick I'm going to die, but I wish to God you would be saved." Mick knew there was no hope but he made out that everything would be alright. People were still on the street running for the city centre. Fear had hit the town. Cars were driving mad and nearly knocking people down. No-one cared about any one. Everything was deserted. Peace and quietness now, and soon this would be all gone. My family were safe. "Mick," I said, crying. "You cry love, what do you want." He was so comforting, how could they kill him? "Can't we go to the church?" "We had better hurry then love, come on." "We'll run to the church." People were in there crying. I looked at Mick. He looked handsome and bold, but he was too kind to be killed. We had only one minute together. The boy I love, would I never see him again? "Lorraine before well . . . before we," he stuttered, "we die together love, you know I love you." This made me cry "I love you too, Mick." Mick started to cry too. He was human he was crying. We held each other tight. We were waiting for death. 10 . . . 9 . . . 8 . . . 7 . . . 6 "I love you Lorraine." . . . 4 . . . "I love you Mick." . . . 2 . . . 1 . . . . . . BANG we knew nothing else . . . . . .

Valerie, 15.

Compared to the hand-to-hand brutality and horror of trench warfare, the war the present generation fights may seem only mental, existential; the struggle to achieve one's identity in the face of

109

ecological breakdown and potential, uncertain nuclear fire. It may also be a part of the social struggle to fight for the conditions which create mutual respect and love for each other. The profiteers who live for established exploitative and hierarchical structures are a formidable enemy, and an enemy inside all of us who necessarily collude and participate in a way of life based on such premises. Jimmy, aged 11, made this point in a poem seeing himself as an unsuccessful pearl fisher who finds his fortune, but also the evil that accompanies such success:

THE PEARL

It's down there, look,
It's glowing . . . Oh, why can't I have it?
I'll jump in,
Oh . . . I've scraped my head on the boat,
How it hurts — it's the pearl,
As I pick it up it's evil.
As I come up the boats are there.
As I look, it sparkles with evil,
The sun reflects off it in my eyes.
My soul hardens, my body hardens,
I am part of the evil now.

Thus as teachers, when we fight any aspect of the present social system, and our emphasis will be on the school system, we are also fighting the parts of ourselves which operate within it. We are all tainted with the system's brutality, and we must recognise and fight the enemy culture, more so when it has been conditioned to exist within ourselves. It is a struggle which we cannot ignore, and when conditions are such that another twelve-year old child writes:

Poor child
Always playing in muddy puddles
Always getting into scrapes and muddles
Poor child

110

Poor child
Dirty clothes, dirty hair
Almost always in welfare care
Poor child

Poor child
Living in the dirty slums of a town
When will they ever pull them down
Poor child

Poor child
Will anything ever be done
Will his time ever come
Poor child

Anon, aged 12.

then it is a struggle that must be pursued and won. With the images
of war all around them, the battery of the media, and the reality of
the conditions against social equality in which many working class
children still find themselves, to fight also means to suffer, for
yourself as well as your connections with other people:

As they wait,
Wait for their enemies to strike again
Lying in wait, hoping they'll win.
Machine guns, rifles,
The noise is terrifying
But if you have to fight, you have
got to suffer.

The wounds are painful
do you know what that means?
It's your turn to die next
although you've done nothing.
The blood is frightening
your wounds are horrifying to look at,
but you know your turn has
come to die.

Pat, 14.

111

The sounds and images of the pop world have become an increasing part of the foundation of imagery for adolescent experience. The people who control the pop world are consequently responsible for the formation of much adolescent imagery and expression. The controllers of this new technology of sound and image, of course, are less interested in the effects of their barrage on the adolescent mind, than they are about the lucrative returns it provides them. So the important question arises: is it possible to use the economic promoters of pop against themselves? Can the images and sounds which sustain the pop profit makers also be used to create the energy and sensitivity to eventually overcome them? If pop is less interested in people than profit, how can adolescent minds turn the exploitative world around them to a human and socialising one?

The folk song of the technological age has become the pop song. Songs are now passed not by word of mouth, but by word and sound of machine and phonograph record. The three minute pop record becomes the standard ballad and image-giver for the adolescent mind. These poems of technology, thrust upon the emerging identity, lay the foundations for symbols and images that can betray it or sustain it. Pop music has also become a background medium, forming a constant accompaniment of sound, image and disc-jockey patter. The level of acceptance of the songs and their symbols often becomes unconscious, unknowing. School-children do their homework to the accompaniment of pop songs and television programmes, and they divide their minds to simultaneously receive and cope with both. This acceptance leads to a parallel acceptance of the symbolism and rhythms of pop songs, and often the sympathy and identification with the singer or the subject of the songs, or the state of mind being communicated.

Pop music can be used to create a genuine education experience. We have to work realistically within the media that are inevitably forming the symbolic structure of the child's expression, in order to fight to reverse its pernicious effects. Pop music is having an enormous impact on adolescent experience. If we work against that experience, we work against the formation of the child's identity at its most vital social stage. There are effects which can stretch the adolescent imagination and help the growth of his understanding of others in situations different to his own. A fifteen year-old boy takes a Manfred Mann hit song, 'My Name is Jack', and creates his own poem, achieving a deep empathy for one of the social rejects of Spitalfields or Whitechapel. He becomes the man through his poem, taking on and confronting a different experience:

My name is Jack
and I live in the back
of a city slum
with rain beating on my back

I was born in the rain
And there I'll probably die,
I may look like a tramp
But this tramp doesn't lie.

I knew a little tramp once
I lent him half a crown
he said, 'I won't forget you, mate'
Now he owns a building in the centre
of New York town.

But for me there is little hope,
Like rain I come and go
I said I'd never told a lie
But my name is really Joe.

Billy, 15.

A fifteen year-old school leaver takes a sentimental song like 'Grandad', and recreates it as a sympathetic insight into the experience of old age, replacing the song's mawkishness with a real understanding:

GRANDAD

'Grandad, Grandad, Grandad'
I hear the kiddies cry.
'Give us a tanner',
Why in my day . . .

No one would cry for sixpence,
It was unheard of,
Only beggars do . . .
I hear my mother cry
'Charlie, dinner's ready . . . '

Oh I was happy way back then
But everyone must grow up
And break away from families.
Oh, how I loved my childhood,
But now it is all gone

I'm brought back to reality
With the kids calling

'Grandad, Grandad, Grandad,
You're dreaming you silly old man,
Give us a tanner an' we'll go away
Grandad, Grandad, Grandad . . . '

Sandra, 15.

Sally, another fourth form leaver, handed me this poem after I'd
been teaching her about a month:

ME

Me, Me and my life,
Me and my life,
Suddenly my life was full
Full of joy and laughter
Suddenly everything was part of
Me, Me and my life
Me, and my life.

Everything seemed out of control
out of control,
by the roll

every, everything out of control
that's Me and My life
Me and My life.

She was talking about her own life, but found that she could grasp
on to the structure of a current hit song to find words and rhythms
to express it. The next poem which she wrote, very soon after,
seemed to use the rhythms of pop music to deepen and intensify the
expression of her experience, as well as confidently assert her
identity:

I walk along the road
Like a Person
A Person
Without love, without care
but I must bear
the Pain of today.

I must think about things
I must live
I must give
I must give what's Mine
but I must bear the
Pain of today.

Using Sally's idea with another class of fourth-formers, I played
several current and past pop records, suggesting that the listeners
wrote their own poems about themselves and their own lives, while
the records were playing. I said that the structures and rhythms of
the songs might help to get them writing, and that some of the
subjects and symbols were ones they already knew well. What
emerged was to me a series of extraordinary poetic statements.
Using the medium with which they could identify most easily —
the popular song — they gave out a whole adolescent world; the love,
the violence, racism, insecurity, solidarity, the struggle for identity.
Although they used the forms and rhythms of various pop songs that
had stayed inside their minds, the song they identified with most
was a Lennon/McCartney song called 'The Long and Winding Road.'

While it was playing, I had found myself writing my own poem on the blackboard; a poem which showed how I, as a teacher trained to 'elaborate' language, found that very 'elaborated' language was taking me too far inside myself. Very often it took the clarity of the children's words to bring me back to the social reality around me:

> The long and winding me
> I twist through my life,
> Meander round a theme I cannot find.
> It's there inside the curves
> And someday I will see
> The long and winding river that is me.

One girl used the song to talk about her boyfriend who was in court that day, up on a charge that could have sent him to Borstal. Some boys saw it as the inevitable football symbol. For other girls, it reflected lost or future love relationships, and for many it became something existential, almost mystical, a symbol which could be grasped as a concreting of adolescent struggle. I later typed up the poems and circulated them around the class as a collective poem, not giving individual names. It is reproduced here. It was a beginning, we were becoming honest with each other, by first admitting honestly what was around us, and what was forming our minds. Commercial pop music had turned to poetry: deflecting and absorbing violence and aggression, promoting sympathy and mutual understanding, and strengthening both individual and collective identities:

THE LONG AND WINDING ROAD

> The long and winding road
> That leads me to the gate
> I will never be free
> Unless I walk this road.
> I'll never go back there
> Never to that gate.
>
> All alone inside a bag,

Not knowing what to do,
Waiting for life to appear before my eyes.
At last my head is out,
And now I can see,
I can see life —
I am only half out
Now my legs are left in,
But now I am out in the world, I can see
    what's going on in the world.
But I cannot move. I am afraid of life.
A hand, a big hand hits me —
I now can move, I now can cry.

When I was born I werent anything
to go mad over.
I must admit I was spoilt right
up to the age of eleven.
After that I sort of grew up.
I'm five foot three, not very fat
nor very nice-looking but looks
arent everything.
Sometimes I think to myself I
wonder how I am going to die or
when I'm going to die.
I then think there is no-one in
this world who is exactly like
me, no-one is because I'm
unique.

I even think that twins and
triplets are each unique in their
own way, that they think different
and do different things.
I think that everything in my body
is keeping me alive and giving me
my imagination and fears, strength,
weakness, these all help me to live.
In my life I will come up against

problems and with any luck
I will overcome this.
I don't fear death because I know
we all have to go sometime.

All my bags are packed
I'm ready to go.
I'm going to say goodbye
I know you won't miss me very much,
I'll still think of you,
Take care of yourself.
We didn't have a long marriage
I knew it wouldn't last long.
Maybe we'll meet again.
Anyway goodbye.

The long and winding road
that leads to the pitch
As we come out the changing
rooms remembering what our
manager said,
Always keep your man
and win the game, don't
stop running for that
ball.

People all said I was ever so nice
that's when I was a baby.
Now I've grown up and keep pet mice
I send my mother half crazy

One day she killed my pet mice
it hurt my heart, I was sorry,
Now that I've run away from home
I don't get no food or lolly

I come back home one sunny day.

I saw my mother a weeping
I run indoors to see what's up
She thought my father was a sleeping
I told my mother, my father he is a dead
I stayed with my mother for ever more,
We lived happy ever after
    that's the story.

Here comes the teams to
play the game,
lead by their captain
who have the brains
They have a kick about before they
starts.
Both the teams are full of
heart, cheer out
la la la la la la la la la la
The Chelsea boys we are
the greatest of all.

Me, I'm my myself
No one in this big
world is like me.
I'm different from you
and everyone else
I'm just plain old
Me.
Me, I'm myself,
No one's like me,
And, I'm not like anyone
I'm just myself
Little old me.
I'm not quite sure what
makes me different
I surpose its in my ways
No one's the same
especialy me.

The long and winding road
Will be for ever closed
If you get put away
Don't go, don't leave me here
I'll never find the way
If you're put inside
Many times I've been alone and
Many times I'm sad
But this will hurt me most
Never to see that road again
The long and winding road
Will be forever closed.

You're always in a world of fantasy
Never looking at things the way there
    supposed to be
You're fluttering through life without a care
And it will never change,
Youre life is a waste of time.

You listen to records but don't take them in
You only see things that aren't there
You're life is easy
Its a waste of time.

I am very tall and skinny
My mates say to me if you
put on a pair of boots you
would look like a golf club.
It makes me take the micky out
of them I say your
midget out of the way I might
tread on you.

I wear glasses to
A lot of my mates take the mick
out of me because I wear
glasses to. They called me goggles

eyed and other names like a
F—————— Blind B———————

I am scottish and my other mate
is irish he always calls me
a F——————— Scotish B———————
So I call him a Irish B———————
But I don't mind I know it's a joke
I don't mind whatever anyone
says to me if only its a joke

My legs are long and are
uncomfortable when I put them
under the desks so I put them
on the chairs but then I hear
the same old cry 'Get your
feet off the furniture lad.' My
legs are useful and all I can
run fast I can reach things
that smaller people can't reach
I think my legs and
arms are very useful.
I think people with short legs
are missing something. If they had
long legs they could reach
something without standing on a
chair and if they have a big
fellow sitting in front of them
in the pictures they could
see over them.
Yes I think every person
should have long arms and legs

Help, I kneed sombody
Help, not just anbody
Cause Ive got my legs stuck
down the drain
Help me if you can I'm really stuck

So get the crain
Help I'll pay anybody just to get
me out this mess
Help the waters seeping through my shoes
I am getting gassed
I never wanted anyone's help
in any way
But now I really do.

Sitting by the window
Having races with the raindrops
Falling down the window pane
Like people in a crowd
Moving about, some going faster
    than others
All meeting at the bottom forming
Crowds of puddles
Sky's all black
Clouds are crying
Once again, Once again
Raindrops down my window pane.

My long and winding life,
Led me to my goal
A long long time ago
Don't leave me standing here
In my old school clothes
It will never disappear
My memory's of long ago
Will lead me to my goal
I've seen that road before
I will change so many years
I will grow so old
And maybe I will die,
But them I would have reached my goal
And I would disappear
I'll never see that road again
That road will lead me there

Right to his door.
The goal I mean is being dead
And the door is Gods house.
As you guest that I'm a ghost
and that I'm very dead
And that's the end of my road
and of my life.

Charlie was a boy who thought he wanted bother
But it went and done him wrong.
Now he dont think its funny cause he went
    and killed a packy
Sitting in the prison cell
Get back
Get back
Get back into your prison cell
Get back
Get back into your prison cell

Now while your sitting idealy by the fire
    side
And your looking at the world through
    darkened glass
Still thinking of the love which we
    have had, but it is now in the past.
Now as the tears begin to fall from my
    eyes
And my make-up is streaming down my
    cheeks
I sit in silence but for the crackling
    fire light.

The long and winding road
That leads to your heart
Will always bring me near
Nearer to your heart.

Time and time again
This road shows the way

The way I'll always find
The way to your love.

But still this road is there
Though the time flickers by
To fast for my love
To find the way.

Every street long and narrow
All the chimneys smoking
Pea soupers around the town
Never a clear day to think of
Just pea-soupers and smoke

Tomatoes are grown on the
        verandas
Potatoes on the allotments
But always the pea soupers.

It was a long dark night
and I nearly had a fright
It was when I saw Ali the pak

It was then the fight began
he had a fry-pan
It was then my friend Dan
stuck an hachet in the back of Ali
the pak

We shoved him in the cut
and then out came his gut
the Canal was polluted with the grease
of Ali the pak.

Any old Rags, any old rags.
At 9 o'clock H.D. Ritchens comes along
    with his horse Ned

With the shout a noise of the hoofs.
No rags today along here Ned
Then the noise slowly seeps
    into the distance.
Any old Rags, any old rags . . . . .

When in time of bovver
Mother Mary sings to me singing words
    of wisdom
put in the boot

When I'm cornered by six blokes
Mother Mary sings to me
Singing words of wisdom
use the axe

In the summer time when the
weather is fine
we—e— have plenty of time
for—r— rolling pakis down the
lane
In the summer time if the time is right
I might get into a great big fight.

Since you've been gone
all that's left is me on my own
No one there to see me home
I'm a lonly child
And the dreams that go through
    my head
leave me alone in bed.

The long and winding road
That's so far away
It lingers on and on
to the long and windy road

so many miles away

No one nos me really, tall
and thin, people take the micky
out of me I laught it off
but really it hurts deep down inside.
I have a lot freinds but really
I have no one I can trust.
I'm not all that peraty and
ant got much of a percanilty
I get frightened quick but
try not to show it.

I think like any one else
I'm rather ordinary.
I tell my mates things I
have not got a lot of secrets.
I worry about life a lot
what people think of
me
I don't think for myself I
try to hide things and kid
myself.
Really I am scared of being
on my own being lonly.
I have lots of feelings
My mum said to much
really
I can't make freinds easy
When I have a chance I
Just chicken out.

The long and winding road
that shows the way to your love
the love I need so much.
I need it so much now.

I see your face in my mind
with the thoughts of love.
The love I love so much,
come to show me the way

Let it be
Let it be
Let it be
yea, let it be
Where is the answer?
Let it be

My street is unbearable to talk about,
It smells of lay-abouts, And
It is filled with chinese and blacks
Everywhere you look
There is a chinese restaurant,
you might as well call it
chinese street, instead of
    Pennyfields Estate.
The smell is getting even
worse with the rubbish,
and the smells is bad
enough with the tramps and layabouts.
And that's what I think of
my chinese, smelly street.

The long and dusty road
when will it ever go?
How long will it last
How long ago did it start
The long and dusty road
When will it ever go?

If only the governors would
give them more money,

Then the dustbin men would
take away the smell.
When will it ever go
When will it ever go
I don't know, but it should go.

Red red blood cumeing from
my head. The blood is over
my face and handes. The axe
is still in my head and my
mate is layeing on the floor
with a axe in his back over
and blood like water is all over him
and around him. The axe had
my blood on it. My mate is
deid but the axe is
still in my head. And a
man came to take the axe out
of me head but I said,
'Let it be, its in me
and not in you.' And I put
me mates' blood in a paper cup
and take it home to have
for some memories of him.
And he was bered in the
back ground of my home.

The long and winding road
that leads from your door
I walk and then I run
along, I can't take any more

You left me once before
by that long and winding road
In my face you slammed the door
I don't want to see that door no more

The wind blows in may face
I turn and walk with grace,
I look back, once more
I'm sorry, I can't take any more.

Let it flow Joe
Let your feelings speak for you
Let the people know what you know.
Tell the people what it's all about
Shout it out.

When you talk people come alive
People start to realise.

Words flow out of your mouth
When you talk about this earth
Tell the people everything Joe
About what you know.

Talk to them Joe.
Let them know
Let the words flow out

In my mind
I think of many things

I think of good things
I think of bad things
My mind is a working machine

When I'm awake its working hard
And when I sleep
Its very quite

My mind is very important to me
My mind is my living machine

I walk, I talk, I run
I am like everybody else.
But I'm me
I am me and me is the thing
I care about
not you but *me*.

I have a brain, but do not use it.
Thats what they all tell me
And I think what a lot of
cods wallop. They're having
a go at me.
I use my brain.
I do what I want to do
Sometimes I talk to myself
and say I'll show them.
I have my secreats.
I am fairly tall
But I will always say I'll show
them all
I use my brain
I do what I want to do
So go stuff yourself one and all.

The long road
Which runs through
Me life
One side runs Love,
the other side runs War
But will it ever end
And people start makeing
friends?
And leave me standing here, the road
in my life?

I'm standing hear looking back on the
long and winding road

Now its all over it was a long time
    ago
I remember walking down that road
    with you
But now I walk alone along that
    road, and the road seems even
    longer now that your gone.

I am Fat and because of that
My mates take the mick,
But I don't care because I take
It out of them. And *when* I catch
Them I give em a good kicking
but only softly so I can Do it
again tomorrow.
I call him egghead or Earholes
when he calls me Bounce.

Every night I go to sleep I have
    a good dream (we say)
Lie down PAK we are going to
    kick your head in
Lie down
You can have the body big footed Joe,
but leave the head to me.
Lie down Pak we're gonna kick yer ead
in lie down
Lie down PAK were gonna kick
it in Kick it in lie down

Nothings gonna change my world
Nothings gonna change my world
I still give the Pakis a good
Kicking
If there six or eight or even
Ten I aint scared I will use
the double barrel or the axe
Nothings gonna change my world

even if I get put in the
nick if there aint no paks,
I do the screws
even if I have only got shoes
and not steels.

Here comes the sun
Here comes the sun
I'll say it all wrong
to keep me from him
because I love him
so here comes the sun
Here comes the sun.

Me, I am myself
By myself all the time
in my home or in the road all time
by myself
People come and people go
but they never come back
to see me again
I am happy, I am sad
and sometimes good and sometimes bad.

I am not like evenbayd
evelyde is togent and
I am all alone
no one comes to see me

The long and winding road
that leads to your mind
will never disappear
I have been in hear before
but a long long time ago,
it always leads me there
I've seen that mind before

but a long long time ago.

Me, Me and my life,
My life is miserable inside, and it
is happy outside.
I get frightened quick and
upset quick.
I was never spoilt
like my sister who is two.
I wish I was the only child,
because of my brother who tells
tales on me.

I, I who have nothing,
I, I who have no-one
Must watch you go walking by
In the arms of another girl,
but it is me who loves you.
You can take her any place you want,
by her fancy clothes and take
her to restaurants.
But you know it is I, who love you.

I was born to think money was everything,
But to some people who have
money, think its nothing.
But to me I have not enough I think.
One week I save to get
Something,
but the next week, I get
something different.

I dream about the wedding,
Fantasy of course,
But a wedding is coming soon —
Fact this time.

Fantasy is so unreal
But its nice to dream
Fact puts the truth to you
So its quite cruel.

People escape to fields of fantasy
Because they can't face the truth,
But, never mind, the time will come
For them to see the facts

Life flies past in a world of fantasy
But in fact it goes quite slow,
So why dream of fantasy
When you have to see the truth someday?

The long and winding Pitch
That Leads me to the Goal
will always be there
Long, Long after im Gone
Will always lead me there
Lead me to the Goal

I see the Sun
Coming from the clouds above,
I see the people's
Happy faces coming back.
I see the Sun
Now it's through
And I keep seeing these pictures of you.

I see the Sun
Going behind a cloud,
I see the people's
Happy faces going wild.
The Sun will soon
Be back I know,
Till then I'll keep seeing these pictures of you.

Out in an open field
With no-one around
I think of lots of fantasy things
Which I wish were going to happen

The hay which is scattered about
Can be the clouds I lay on
The sky which is up above
Can be a sea below.

The long and winding road
that leads to this school
will never disappear I've seen that road before
it always leads me hear leads me to this school
I came here a long long time
ago
Why do I have to come, come
to this school

but still it leads me back to the long and
winding road I came down hear a long long time
ago, dont keep me in this school lead me to
the door

The words quoted in this book are working-class words:
adolescents speaking about their own world in their own language,
sometimes borrowing symbols, but always applying them to their
own life-situation. Since Professor Basil Bernstein revealed his
insights concerning language and class, much has been made of
'elaborated' and 'restricted' codes of language, and much has been
said of 'compensating' working class children for their 'restricted'
speech patterns. It has been seen as the task of the teacher of English
to carry his working class children through school English lessons*

* Harold Rosen has also made this point, in a lecture on Bernstein at
the History Workshop on *Children's Liberation* at Ruskin College,
Oxford, April 1972. (Published as *'Language and Class'* by Falling
Wall Press, 79 Richmond Rd., Bristol, BS6 5EP).

towards the 'elaborated' standards of language which Bernstein identifies with middle class life. But to elaborate is not necessarily to clarify, it is sometimes more likely to complicate and often to confuse. One of the great masters of middle class, elaborated standards of English himself wrote:

> *Words are like leaves; and where they most abound*
> *Much fruit of sense beneath is rarely found.*

Alexander Pope.

The direction away from the clarity and simplicity of working class words towards middle-class language standards, is also a carriage towards the middle class life, values and habits. As Bernstein has shown us, it means a great emphasis on individuated rather than group expression. This encourages a movement away from verbal solidarity towards verbal self-indulgence. It is the movement from what is normally and pejoratively called 'common' to what is called 'proper', — both epithets being value judgments from middle class standards. The movement from 'restricted' code to 'elaborated' code also gives more expression to abstraction rather than concrete reality, removing language further and further from the social facts, and taking it closer towards fantasy, illusion and mystification.

The teacher of English must stand up and affirm the working class loyalties of the language that his students speak. He must not accept those judgments pronounced by an alien culture upon his own culture and the culture of the children he teaches, but move towards establishing criteria developed through the culture of their own social class and belongingness. A language of clear insight, empathy and solidarity is not a restricted code of language, but an unbounded code of language. Words which inspire generosity and shared experience, people speaking together and solidarising, affirming themselves and their class, are the words which constitute a truly educational language. These are the words of the language of identity, not the language of alienation.

Consequently, poetry, for working class children, does not become so much a distillation of words, forced through the mental and linguistic energy of reducing elaboration and making unnecessary words redundant as it tends to with middle class language users. It is more a direct and truthful observation and commentary on their

experience of the social relationships and concrete reality of their
world, with so many of the facts weighted against them. Any fantasy
that does occur may well be a deliberate escape from confronting the
facts of social injustice all around them. Words of working class
identity force a realisation of their position in the world, and their
oppressed life-situation:

When you talk people come alive
People start to realise . . .

The poetry stays factual, close to the streets, without illusions. D.J.
Enright, a poet himself, writing in the very middle class literary
journal, *Encounter**, found the poetry of these children very
threatening:

But what is inescapably painful, and frightening, about these
laconic verses, and finally most impressive, is the children's
clearsightedness, their unwavering gaze — or at any rate, their
total absence of illusions.

And he quotes from Sandra's poem, to tell himself why:

Fantasy is so unreal
But it's nice to dream.
Fact puts the truth to you
So it's quite cruel.

People escape to fields of fantasy
Because they can't face the truth
But never mind, the time will come
For them to see the facts . . .

The working class words which tell of this 'unwavering gaze' and
understanding of social fact and social injustice, and the solidarity
with which they are generally communicated through working class
language are enough of a threat to warrant the enemy culture to
lure working class children away from their own language standards,
and persuade them through the schools towards the divided and

confused standards of middle class elaboration. The strength of working class resistance to the absorbtion of its values and vision by the middle class culture, must be maintained and mobilised by the teacher of English, who must protect and nourish the language of his students. When doing this, he will find that he has found the side of his students, and is sharing their words, their mutual belongingness, and sharing their lives.

THREE BOYS

'Among the crimes there is innocence'

Intiaz Ahmed Malek.

1. JIMMY

Jimmy lives in a council flat in Shadwell, alongside the overhead
railway which runs from Fenchurch Street in the city, out to
Southend. His father is a docker, and there are seven children in the
family. I met him as a member of a fourth-form class which I taught.
His class was called 4R, a non-examination class, all of whom were
expected to leave at fifteen, at the end of their fourth year. They
were an unpredictable class, sometimes voluble and friendly,
sometimes sullen and aggressive. For them, '4R' meant '4 Rejected',
and they knew it. They were at school to fill the weeks before they
could legally leave, and their teachers were supposed to keep them
quiet, and keep them amused. They had no enthusiasm for school,
although very often they loved to talk and joke.

For them, the exercise of 'writing' was only seen as a drill, a
forced act, an act of self-oppression, 'writing' was unnatural. It was
an exercise that had been imposed on them from the moment they
entered school, and now, so near to their release, they could reject it
and refuse to do it. Their act of refusal was a last rebellious act. At
the last juncture of school they were saying, 'Now I will not serve.'
But gradually, through writing some poetry and responding to their
own world, they did begin to write again: all except Jimmy.

I tried to encourage him, cajole him, persuade him with every
approach I knew, but he would not write a word. I knew that he
could write both fluently and grammatically, as I had seen some of
his previous work, but now in his last months, he would not write
in my classes. Locked inside a low stream all through his school life,

this defiance was a firm and clear gesture against the school's idea of language and expression. He would only sit at his desk and doodle, not speaking very much to anyone, only looking very bored and very wasted. In one lesson, he saw a photograph of a local church, St. Anne's, Limehouse, with its strange and ornate 17th Century Hawksmoor tower. He asked if he could draw it, and spent three lessons in absolute concentration, trying to capture its complicated proportions. After he finished, one of the girls in the class, Gillian, wrote a poem about the church, and then copied it across the top of Jimmy's picture, making a marriage of word and image. After that, Jimmy drew all the time, every lesson, making pictures to which the others would add their words.

These were 'English' lessons, the realm of 'the word'. For Jimmy, there was a sense of liberation in this drawing. He had always drawn, but never much at school. When I went to his home, I saw that his whole family were artists. His elder brother had huge portfolios of his own work. The boys' bedrooms had been painted and decorated by themselves, with strange and orginal patterns on the walls and ceilings. The little sister grasped hold of my visit as an opportunity for a drawing, and drew a picture of me. Jimmy's father, back from the docks, sat in his chair and was criticising and complimenting the family artists. With his wife, he kept a close and intelligent eye on everything the children drew and painted, bought them paint and materials, and encouraged their work in every way he could. When I was there, he was criticising the wide lips that Jimmy tended to draw on some of his faces, and they were trying to work out a more efficient technique together. He was proud and pleased at the skill and enthusiasm of the family's work. The flat shone with art and a keenness to create.

Seeing Jimmy in school the next day, in an atmosphere that gave only dullness and boredom, I could only curse to myself. How much was the school failing this boy? If only that family love and encouragement could come through these iron gates and walk along these corridors. Why had he been insulted by vicious grading all the way through his school life? Why had he been forced towards words when his natural form was images, lines and shapes? Words were at last beginning to come from him now that his identity was being established through his pictures. Now he was writing and drawing, but it was towards drawing that he moved with love. Like tens of thousands of adolescents, he had to establish himself in a peculiar,

She holds him tightly,
Tears rolling down her cheeks
She thinks this may be the last
time she will see him.
gone, gone for ever,
In to a different world,
New people, new home,
then she kisses him
and slowly he wa'
away.
Into the dark and lon
Street.

by
KATHLEEN
LEIG

positive way, a way which made him different and recognisable.

Jimmy left school as soon as he could after his fifteenth birthday, and now works in a butcher's shop in Watney Street, Stepney. His school never recognised him. It left him unrealised and unfulfilled, even in his own modest expectations of himself.

2. INTIAZ AHMED

I came over to England six years ago. Before I
came I lived in a bungalow. It was a good clean
place with a garden and from near by I could see
a river with sand beach and a few coconut trees
and date trees. There was a bridge there too,
it was a springy bridge. I used to go down there
sometimes with the other people I knew there. We
used to climb trees and enjoy the sunshine.

When we come to England, I did not know how to
feel, sad or happy because I had to leave the
sunshine and friends and happy life and I thought
about coming here I thought it would be better.
It would be good to see cars all day and live in
high buildings and enjoy playing in the snow.

When I got off the plane, cold air hit me, I didn't
mind, in a way I like. It was a good feeling to
come into the cold from hot weather. I was a bit
disappointed when I saw the place where I had to
live for the next part of my life. Anyway, we got
into the house. I was surprised to see what met my
eyes, paper walls, no fans, a bright light, my dad
went over to a box, he just touched it, he moved
back, and the box slowly came to life, it was
television.

The house is good from the inside, not the outside.
I accepted the facts. I had to accept.

Intiaz lived in a decaying square just north of St. Katherine's Docks. From his roof, Tower Bridge loomed large, and the derelict docks sprawled beneath. Half his buildings were themselves derelict and condemned, and his family were waiting to be rehoused. Later, after he had moved, he had a strange vision of the last moments of the life of his old home:

ROYAL MINT SQUARE

The dark and dreary place
Pulled down from existence

Its happy sparks nearing the dynamite

Old people dying
With this unhappy world of Royal Mint Square

The merciless dynamite explodes
Pulling the body of the square apart.

He was the only Asian boy in his class, and lived in an area where Asians were seen as unwelcome and interloping. In the months of 'Paki-Bashing' he became threatened and isolated. He was different, and he knew this and lived this, it was only one of the 'facts' he had to accept. One day in class, in response to a Ron McCormick photograph of some doors imposed under the dark and bleak arches below the railway at Shoreditch, he wrote this poem:

Time and distance
They both travel equally
Waiting for no one
Time is sometimes wasted
Time is sometimes fastened
The green grass is taken by time
    as time goes into the future
And makes it present and the grass
    is polluted.

Sometimes people are left behind
   by time, when people are old
   the time leaves them.
The world and its people get old
But time goes on and on.

He was hidden away in mid-school in a class called 3C, a boisterous group full of laughter and high spirits. Intiaz' serious and searching vision was completely foreign to that atmosphere. He grasped abstracts and concepts which few of his classmates could understand or sympathise with. Finding himself with words, and discovering a vessel into which he could pour his unique identity, he began to write many short pieces mostly on small pieces of paper, which he would quietly slip to me. Each one seemed a part of a commentary on himself:

Look skywards
The sun is going red
It's old now,
cold and lifeless,
A lone person
Shouts,
Nobody answers
everything is still
Tranquil like it used
to be

THE CELLS

Among the crimes there is innocence
Among the bad there is Good
Through Injustice Justice stood
Through the dark Hell
Brightness shone,
Dimness of Space
Brightness of Earth
Darkness of death
Brightness of light

Last moments to death,
Step out to gunfire,
 Order to lie in the hills of death,
As you step out.
First gunfire, then intense silence
No visions,
No Body,
Can't move,
Just floating away
is that the mercy of God
After life on Earth?

Came like the thunder
Gone like the wind
A person's speedy life
is passed
Our dim planet is dark Gloomy
and silent

Every dark gloomy alley was silent
No one moved, everybody
lay silent on the floor
The End has Come,
The doomed planet circles the
Sun forever.

It was as if he was trying to articulate and drive out from himself some strange, apocalyptical spirit that was tormenting him. His mind, he knew, was not like English minds. It was full of Asia and Islam, with ideas and images that came from a foreign land to speak about a new identity in Stepney. One poem he wrote spoke about 'Dim dark nature':

Nature's dim dark future
Past is gone
Nature's gone too,
Present is passing
Dim dark nature dissolving too

future is bright
but only for fright
Dim dark nature.

'Nature', he said, looking around his crumbling square, 'Well, it's all this concrete, isn't it?' The decay and concrete death all around him, married with his fascination for space and the future. His poetry saw the apocalypse as something terrifyingly real. The devastation and dereliction of the area where he lived was not far away from his stark images of barrenness and destruction. It was as if his Asian eyes were seeing a broken, crumbling London identity all around them:

Timeless
Godless
Savages that lurk in the deepest universe
Shapeless paradise their home
Gases they breathe
Cyanide they eat

The mood of deep melancholy and isolation in his poetry was not unrelated to his social situation. The first time I called into his flat to talk to Intiaz' parents about his poetry, his father, now working on Paddington station, said I was the first Englishman, in nearly six years since he had been in the country, who visited his home, who wasn't there on official business. No one from the school had ever been there. This was the 'pastoral care' which the school was so proud of. In that dim flat, closed in by decaying brick, the flame of Intiaz' and his family's heroism and strength became suddenly inseperable from the force and final optimism of his poetry:

The Earth drags on, heavier and heavier by the ever growing
    population,
Our star begins to lose its shine.
Grandfather's clock ticks on leaving its owner to rot.
No one wants to wait, listen and look at themselves

or what they are doing to what is around them.
At last they become old and slow and are left behind
    by the new generation,
Like a new bulb from an old powerhouse.

He was far less sure writing prose than he was writing poetry, but after some persuasion, he began to write his autobiography:

AUGUST 11 1957

In the morning of a rare rainy day, in August, calculated time eight a.m., was born I.A. Malek, just another human come to increase the population of the underdeveloped country called India. And that person is the author of this passage, writing the precise moments fourteen years after his arrival on earth. Born near the coasts of the Indian ocean, in the city of Baroda, commonly, high populated. I was born in a well-mannered house, where money was a small problem, this prosperous place did not belong to my father, who was an engine driver, earning 60 shilling (80 pence) a month. (The house belonged to his brother & we lived there). He was always a littel exhausted (owing to night shifts), but full of inthusiasm & curiosity. He always thought and said about reaching higher and firmer grounds.

SEPTEMBER 1966

I was nine years old approxamatly, I did not know the shape of the world then, and could not place a plane from a duck. In early august of 1966 a.d. we were to come to England, in a 727 (air India) plane. I wasn't in the least excited, I did not know what a plane was. Late afternoon of the following week we arrived at the airport. The air vessels greatly fasanated me. I had not seen an aircraft from such minor distance. I was to get even closer by the time evening arrived. The deep round red body of Sol was disappearing from the Horizon of India, when the aircraft lifted for its destination.

NOVEMBER 1966

Everyday a grey one, days passing like minutes. House
instead of stones seemed to be made of damp paper.
porpousless objects. Despite all these facts, I was alive in this
country. It represented Science, knowledge and the true shape
and place of the earth. It represented size of the UNIVERSE,
the Countless billions of Suns, Solar Systems, & civilizations.
Weeks passed each & everyday eventless, when one day dad
brought home a telivsion, which brightened up the evenings.
I watched the glowing box everyday, correction, evenings.
What interested me was a baldy man who appeared at 6 and
9 five days a week, much later I found out he was a
newscaster, and strangely named 'Gordon Honeycomb'.

AUGUST 1967

THE ROYAL MINT SQUARE (PRIVATE LODGING)

A small portion of my life was given to these slums, half good
and half miserable. I shall never forget these weird but kind
buildings, I learned the two sides of English socity there,
which were unually different from each other.

SCHOOL FROM 1968-71

Half my primary days I was the bass, turning slowing to
stupid brutellness. The other half taught me otherwise. At
the age of eleven I accepted secondary school unhappily,
my first year a quiet peaceful eventless term passed with ease,
I was happy for first time since I had come to england.
But that happiness went as suddnely as it came, and that
happyness went so far it took two years to reach it. I lost my
happyness because I was smarter now and was transferred to
one 'c'. Here I was alone, locked, shut up in a doorless cabin,
with a ray of rescoue two years away. The teacher was a small
slightly on the fat side always had a smile. I seem to fit in with
five boys all 'skinheads'. It all went well while that teacher was

around. By the time a new teacher arrived in 3C the class had turned destructive, against all the learners. In this span of time came in a boy named 'hussey' who seemed angel from heaven, but he, after a few days, no, months appeared to be devil sprouted up from the hell.

Days later another boy named 'John Goatham' nicknamed, 'James Kirk', becuase he liked star trek and looked liked the film star, arrived. He started talking to the class one by one since no one paid any attention to him he turned to talk to me, I got mixed up with him, and never regretted a moment of it. The class got to 'NOVA' Destruction point. Joined and pushed in the right direction they were capable of doing a lot of damage to the school.

Here I did not wish that I wasn't born but that I wished I never come on earth. I distinctly remember saying that to the world in general. After saying that I kept thinking why I did, and all around to see if anybody heard.

THE TURN

When I was nearing the end of third year, it was nine months, approx. 252 days or 36 weeks, I remember this much, because I kept counting days and school hours minutes & sometimes even seconds, thinking that that second will not arrive again, ever, in eternity or after. Time will never repeat itself, I grow old and vanish from peaple's minds, never to live or feel the air and breath of life, but I realized its foolishness to think of death before you were nearing dead. Anyhow a new teacher arrived to take drama classes, to the head an enemy who'se to be shot on sight, to the pupils of 3C a chance for a laughter. But in that drama class, I learned to explain myself. A poem I wrote proved itself imagative to the teachers to me a half cut reality. It got places, I got a slice of publicity which was my third fantasy, two of which I still want, but logic proves I will never get. That poem expressed full force of my Brain and transford to a better line of class. 4GA.

But I know I will not stop their, I will move on to better things which will make this place look like trase from the Dustbins.

Intiaz Ahmed's talent and experience was a part of a level of life that had always been considered un-English. In his 'C' stream class, isolated by his Asian identity, he had somehow not been seen as a contender for the successes of the English school system. His unsure grammar and spelling, and uncategorisable imaginative skills had dropped him to the side of the school mainstream. His mind was peculiar, abnormal to the British middle-class educational norms, and there seemed no place for it unless it accepted them and adopted them. A successful education for him would be seen as the breaking of his identity by the force of British educational chauvinism.

Intiaz Ahmed has now stopped writing poetry, and is getting on seriously with his C.S.E.s, drilling his mind to forget its uniqueness. There is no G.C.E. or C.S.E. in his identity, only in the new facts which he must now assimilate in order to succeed. If the drilling and sterility of the next few years' education takes away his poetry, it will be an assassination. As Intiaz says, the 'facts' he had to accept, but those 'facts' are created by economic power, organisations and interests. This boy, as all citizens, must have his share in creating, changing and re-shaping the 'facts' all around him, and not merely obey them and submit himself to them.

3. BARRY

Barry's mother is white, from Holland Park: his father is a black musician from St. Lucia. They lived in Spitalfields:

I live in a block of flats it isn't a high block it is only a four storey block. I like it where I live, their are lots of boys their just my age and over (14). Sometimes I hate it because there is a factory over the road from where i live, you would be surprised when i say factory you would say that there is no harm in a factory but when you tell them what sort of factory they will be so ashamed to live their. The factory is no ordanary one it is a chicken factory. not only that it is the smell alone, which smells like a sewer. My family is moving this time next year because our flats are being modernised, by that time we would have saved up to have our own house. No one in my area like it not even my family, none of her friends come up for a cup of tea because of the smell wicht turns them off.

The people are lazy on my landing they will not even clean the stairs or sweep the landing, every time my mum or my (16) year old sister does it. They have got plenty of space for houses because they have knocked a lot of old ones down, but instead they are just building car parks all the time. We have got a football pitch behind the flats but it is so small you could not play a five aside properly. We have all asked the council for a new one but they just say next month some one will be round to see it — that was about 2 years ago.

Most of the area is a slum district and every were you go it either smells of chickens being killed or burnt or in another way being slautered but their is a smell you can't get rid of and that is the pakistanis, the smell of curry and goodness nos what you canot get rid of the smell and their is a discusting habit in black lion yard and that is the Junkies that take drugs, the police go round their every day and take one or two away for drugs. The little children see this and when they hide there drugs so the police can't pick them up they go and take them. But now it all cleared up. But we still do not like the area we are living in it is a discrase to London, all of the people who live in the block of flats that i live in never take any notice of what is bieing said and done. I for one thing it is discousting how they kill chickins, They grab them by the legs and cut the necks with a razor, but some of this isn't bad to the way I have seen other people do it. Some cameramen come round and take films of the slums and put actors in it, their is one programme on television which is called (Never Mind the Quality feel the Width) (starring patric many and Many Cohen). They have done this film in a bombed house and taken some shots from Whitechapel and other places to make it look good, so others for that district is alright etc.

Barry was another fourth form leaver, in the same class as Jimmy. He had come up the school in the same hard way, through a low-

streamed class. He was always unsettled and unpredictable, he
hated sitting still, and hated being kept quiet. He rarely concentrated
his mind on writing, but when he did, his concentration was very
profound. There were many things on his mind: his family, his area,
and his whole life-situation as a brown-skinned boy in a
neighbourhood where one boy in every three reaches the juvenile
courts before he is eighteen. There was always at least one of his
friends in trouble with the police, and he was often picked up and
handled roughly by them, because of the inevitable association and
expectations of his life-situation. His skin too, became another
factor:

> I live in a block of flats where people
> do play I have no friends day after day
> if I have no friend I can't play
> So I stay in and look after myself.
> I noticed they started to talk to
> Me it was becuase I was black
> and they were just saying to theirselves, let's speak
> don't be rotten

My problem as a teacher was, how do I, from a different world,
come to terms with this boy's experience, expectations and past
history? What could I do to at least make an effect, when his whole
life had been an education of shock, frustration and repression. He
started writing poems. He picked up an idea from the devastated
sites all around his buildings which had been made into car parks. He
said he was imagining that he was a local housing officer, full of
guilt for the offical preference of cars to people:

> I like to live in a house
> where there is space
> we knock down houses
> and we build car parks
> Why don't we build houses?
>
> My conscience keeps pricking me

I don't know what to do
except build car parks
'I wonder why?'

He began to write about himself through the experience of pop
music. He seemed to scream out through the images and rhythms
that were all too familiar to him:

I never had a dream
come true. So for once in
my life I just want a dream
to come true.

People changed but dreams
still stay the same without
someone else about the
house so let it be so true

Then my dream will
come true
I hope not before the
time I die I'll mash
my dreams to pieces.

I am standing here looking back
on the long and winding road

it was a long time ago,
I wish I was alone
but not on the widening road

the road seems longer
now you're gone so come
back and shorten it
please I am just helpless

I was doing everything that the liberal, concerned teacher should do for him, but it amounted to nothing. I was taking him out, visiting and talking with his parents, getting him to read his poetry in public, getting it published, even getting him to read it on television. I was constantly encouraging him, talking to him, but ultimately the only thing I could do for him would have been to have found him a good lawyer. As a 'teacher' I was impotent. His education had already happened, and education of bruises, cuts and scars, far truer than my liberal, literary one that I was offering him at school. It spoke for him, and thousands like him. It told him he was part of a 'criminal' class, 'prone' to getting into trouble, and therefore socially treated as such, with only disrespect, deprivation and rejection, being pushed into side alleys by the police, threatened, insulted and beaten. These were his social expectations. He has since had a series of court appearances, and is now on remand, waiting for another case to be made against him. He is a kind and intelligent boy, with a fire of compassion and sensitivity which was never allowed to be kindled. He wrote this poem about a quest his mind once took. His journey frustrated, he still feels and loves:

MY KITTEN

On Friday 9.30 a.m.
I Heard a kitten cry
I went looking for it
It was in a tree across a river
I wondered how it got there.
So I swam across
but it was no good
the current was drawing me away
I wish I was in a boat
Then I was shouting for help
no one heard me
I was just going over then I fainted
When I woke up the dock attendant said
'I saved your life'
so I thanked him and said,
'I have to be on my way
I am going to save a kitten.'

'Where is it?
What colour is it?'
'It is black', I said.
'You nearly died for that kitten.'
Then he said,
'It was my kitten it always goes up there.'
So then he sat down and cried.
I said
'Don't cry.'

Barry has gone from a rejected stream in a secondary school to a room in a remand home. He has been passed from the Department of Education and Science to the Home Office, from teachers to police. The collusion between education and the law, the schools and the courts, acting as an axis against particular children from particular 'crime prone' areas, only exposes the function of both, to preserve a social and political status-quo against the working class child. In a generation that has known the lives and fates of George Jackson, Stephen McCarthy and Jake Prescott, Barry's words speak to us with utter conviction. We know we will not continue to accept these brutalities running through our institutions:

I can't remember the date when I arrived but ever since it has been boring it is still because my friend has gone home. It is better than some places that I can think of. The police have warned me before that they will get me since I made an allegation against a policeman.

156

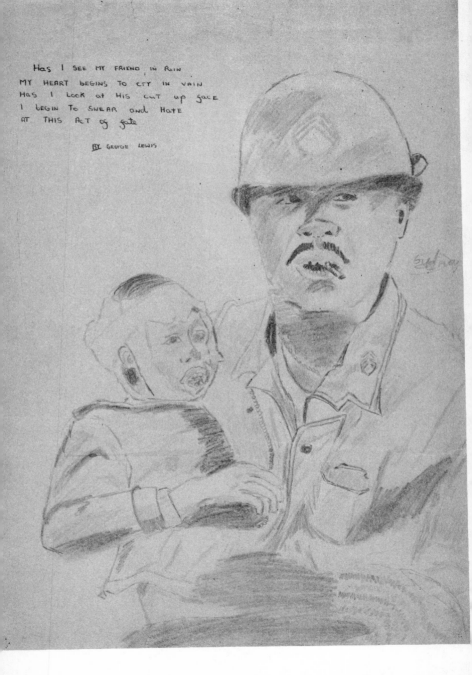

Has I see my friend in ruin
My heart begins to cry in vain
Has I look at his cut up face
I begin to swear and hate
at this act of fate

By George Lewis

The last time that I went to court and got off a policeman said that they will get me on anything they can, so now they are trying to frame me for a stabbing I didn't do. I don't like being locked up for something I never done, so that the police can laugh at me as if they have got away with it. They have told me to move out of the east end district but I am not going to let them terrorise me for the fun of it.

There is a house master here that doesn't like the black's he never starts on the white kids here is an example on the 25/5/72 I had to go to court but the night before all the white boys were running around about 3 O'clock in the morning and he started taking it out on the blacks he couldn't take it out on me because I was going to court but when I came back he locked me in (CP) close provision for 24 hours and that night I never done a thing it's not my fault that I am half black and half white . . .

Barry wants to join the army. He says by doing that he can escape the London magistrates, he can still go to Ulster. So now it will be from Spitalfields to Ulster, to fight other young working class men trapped like himself, to kill or to be killed, like the young blacks in the southern states of the U.S.A., escaping only to kill their counterparts and potential comrades in Vietnam. For the teachers of all these boys, it is insufficient to be only a teacher. The only chance for boys like Barry is not education or rehabilitation. It is a new society with new democratic, socialist values and equal care for everyone. Unless the teacher carries with his books his ideas and commitment for a complete social change, he is doing nothing but teasing and lying to his children.

LET'S HAMMER ON

My future, what is it?
Or is that too much a question
   that my mind can't function
   to answer.
It's that open space that every-
   one looks into.
We step forward a pace.
Leave past and present and
   concentrate on the future.
The thing I must penetrate,
And put up, against patience.
But I
Must use the patience to
   withstand the suspense of what
   my future holds.
Not me, you, or anyone can
   tell you what you're waiting
   for.
You'll never reach your peak.
Future!
Future is infinity
That goes on and on.
It never ends until one gives
in, and it's you.
It grows old, you die.
And never can you tell what
   you once had, but you never
   did find out what it was
   you were seeking.

                    Sharon, 11.

When I'm a man
I bet I can
Climb a montain and
fly to Japan.
ride every racing
car ride into space
and finish my tea
without jam on my face.

Jackie 4 R.

BEFORE THE FIGHT

With heaving breasts and heavy chests
We hammered on till day was nigh,
Regardless of the Satan thread
Of hosts to meet us bye and bye,
And why should we be opposed by a savage foe?
Why can't we decide our destiny?
We've been beacons of light
To civilisations before tonight.
Gentlemen!
Let's hammer on.

John Crowe

The schools' inspector who inspected me in my class in Stepney, told me that the function of the teacher there was to work towards a situation where the children would 'transcend' their environment. The middle class bias of the schools offers a choice to the working class child: 'transcend', or be consumed, move upwards, away from your origins and join the middle class, or fall back and join the labour market. A working class child can either become mindful of the hierarchy and start climbing, or accept his position and be endlessly exploited, endlessly consumed. The only other alternative is struggle. The machine does not stop for individuals going through it, only for the people who operate and control it. The realisation amongst children of the boredom and futility of a school life which only moulds them into labour fodder, can create a cynicism and despair which makes an intelligent twelve-year old girl write as if all was decided and finished already:

THE WOURLD IS DIM AND DULL

My class room is dim and dull
My teacher sits there thinking

She's so dim and dull
that she just sits there thinking

The wourld is dim and dull
my life is not worth liveing

Now many school students are staying on at school not merely to get
qualifications but to build up a strong union movement. School has
become an area of struggle for them, their activity at school, the
syllabus of struggle. They are becoming subjects of their own destiny
and not objects or receptacles for alien knowledge. From all over the
country children in schools have a growing consciousness of their
exploitation, of their being used as political pawns in a game by the
profit makers. The formation of their own unions has given them a
huge solidarising energy.

Children from a working class situation have an obvious empathy
and recognition for the state of the working class man. Maxine's
poem about a lonely dustman expresses strange insights into the
nature of oppression and release. A dustman's livelihood is his
rubbish, which he must treat brutally, although he owes a debt to the
rubbish which gives him his job. And it is the same with the social
and political system, which, dependent on its working class children
for its survival and maintenance, treats them with little respect and
gives them no choice. The teacher, society's agent in the schools, is
like the lonely dustman. Dependent on the children for both his
raison d'être and his raw material, he takes them from the dark
world of the school to the darker world of the dead-end job or the
dole, and yet his liberalism still likes to make him see them as his
friends:

I, the lonely dustman, go walking along the
    dusty streets, my only truthful friends
    are the rubbish.
They come rushing against me, so that I can throw
    my only friends away into a world of
    rubbish.
Every day my friends are thrown into the streets
    and put into iron cages,
And they rely on me to take them out of a dreadful,
    dirty and awkward world of horror.

162

Then along comes a different world.
It's a dust-cart.
Then once more my friends rush against me
 and I throw them into a world of darkness.
But now we are on strike, I see my friends
 wherever I go.

The fact is that we are all workers: teachers, children, parents, and children themselves can soon identify with oppressed and exploited adults. The teacher of English affirms his class allegiances to his children by stimulating creative empathy and solidarity with other sections of the oppressed. Two twelve-year old East End boys extend themselves to the mines:

THE MINERS

JACK   Nice morning, hant it Stan?

STAN   Yes, loverly morning. Don't really fancy going down the mine today.

JACK   Has your wife had her baby yet Stan?

STAN   No, not yet.

JACK   I am sure that them pit props were craking last week, Stan.

STAN   Better not tell Mr. Simons Jack, you know he don't like fussy men.

JACK   I don't care. I think someone's got to tell him before we all get killed.

STAN   But does that someone have to be you?

JACK   Well I don't think none of them silly boys down the mine will.

STAN   Now don't get to hasty. Remember they have to work just has hard as you do.

JACK   I don't care. I am going right now to see that Simons bloke, and tell him what I think of him and his crumby mine and I don't care if I lose my job.

STAN   Mind what you say Jack, they say he's a very hard bloke to talk to. I know you don't have a wife and kids to support like me, but what about your old mum?

JACK   I never thought of it like that.

STAN	Well, Jack, you will never find another job this side of Wales when he tells all the mine owners what a trouble-maker you are.
JACK	Your right I suppose, but I just wish there was something I could do.
STAN	Well there's nothing, Come on, let's go down the mine, we're late already.
JACK	O.K. Stan, but one of these days I'll tell that money-pinching miser.
STAN	Save it. Till next time.

That the two writers are 'children' is irrelevant. They have recognised a parallel political situation to their own political situation. If one of them were to step out of line at school, or confront the hierarchy, he would also be victimised, blacklisted. The same would be true for their teachers. If they recognised their teacher as a worker like the miner, or like themselves, rather than an enemy like the miner's boss — they would also identify with his struggle against the employers and the interests that are exploiting him. They would begin to see the teacher as a friend, a comrade like the miner, and not a foe. Then the most damaging division of school life might begin to heal.

As children can extend their imaginations to involve themselves in the political struggle of older people, so older people can remember their own struggles of the past when they were young and joined together to stop brutality as it marched towards them wearing black shirts. A 65-year old lady remembers:

OCTOBER 1936

We stood at Gardiner's Corner,
We stood and watched the crowds,
We stood at Gardiner's Corner,
Firm, solid, voices loud.

Came the marching of the blackshirts,
Came the pounding of their feet,

Came the sound of ruffians marching
Where the five roads meet.

We thought of many refugees
fleeing from the fascist hordes,
The maimed, the sick,
The young, the old,
Those who had fought the fascist lords.

So we stopped them there at Gardiner's,
We fought and won our way.
We fought the baton charges,
No fascist passed that day!

Milly Harris, 65.

Many of the poems quoted in this book were first published in a small anthology called 'Stepney Words'. I was a teacher in a Church of England secondary school in Stepney, and it soon became very obvious to me that the children in my classes were producing moving and important poetry, full of insights about themselves, their neighbours, their class position, their streets and buildings, their whole world. One day, while my mind was fastened on these poems, I happened to be walking past Whitechapel Library, when I noticed there was an exhibition showing there the work of a young local photographer called Ron McCormick. In Ron's photographs of the streets and people of Spitalfields and Whitechapel, there was the same compassion, the love, the extension of the self, and the social profundity that I had seen in the children's poetry. Through this photographs he had captured a few streets, a village in a city, but a whole world. I wrote a note saying how much I admired the photographs, and that I was a local teacher whose pupils had written many clear sighted and empathetic poems which I would like him to see. In my mind, already his photography and the children's poetry were marrying.

He came to see me the next day and read the poetry. We talked a lot about the area, the poetry, the insights of the children's words and his photographs, and I invited him to bring some of his photographs to school the next week, to give back to the children their own world through his eyes and his camera. He also superimposed some of the poems on huge blown-up prints which we produced to show the poets at school. Ron was welcomed by the children at school, and we spent the day with different classes, talking about the photographs and the people and buildings they depicted, encouraging the children to write directly from ideas which the photographs generated in them. From this experience the idea of 'Stepney Words' was born. We approached the Headmaster of the school, and asked him if the school or its Governors would be prepared to sponsor the idea of an anthology of the children's poetry, illustrated by Ron McCormick's photography. We had no money: I was a probationary teacher, and Ron was a student. The Headmaster seemed to like the idea, so we began to think about the anthology, and showed the poetry to as many people living in the community as we could. We met in pubs, in cafés, in our flats, talking to parents, to the children themselves, and anyone else who wanted to contribute to the idea. We produced a draft anthology and gave it to the Headmaster, who showed it to the school Governors. He told us the next day that the Governors didn't like it, that they considered too many of the poems 'drab', and the anthology generally 'unbalanced'. I subsequently heard that they had a special dislike for this poem, written by a fifteen-year old boy who had adopted the argot of his own streets and his own identity to express in his poetry something of the extent of his own and his friends' class expectations:

Mum!
cried the boy
who wanted attention.
Mum!
cried the boy
who was lonely and cold.
Dad's gone out boozing
we're all on our own.
She punched him in the mouth
and told him 'shuddup,
I'm watchin' the tele
leave me alone.'
It's the same every night.

Me dad's on the booze
Me mum's watching tele.
They won't let me go out
'case I get in trouble.
The old man got nicked
for rapin' some woman.
Gord nose what'l 'appen
When he gets his conviction
We'll 'ave no money
'cos another's in the oven.
Anyway,
Movver won't go out to work.

Chris, 15.

They asked me to re-structure the anthology, leaving out poems
thought too 'drab' and all the photographs. I said that if the
Governors didn't like the anthology, that was up to them, but we
would find the money amongst ourselves and our friends and other
people in the local community, to finance the anthology. But the
Headmaster said the Governors 'would not allow' the publication of
any poems written by children of the school, unless they had
financial control over the anthology. It seemed like a deadlock, and
Ron and myself were both angry and surprised. I was later ordered
not to publish the anthology.

There seemed to us to be more important things at stake than the
unreasonable instructions of school governors, most of whom did
not live in the area. We had a commitment to the children, to whom
we had promised to publish their poems, their parents, our
neighbours, and the whole local world of which we were a part. So
we went ahead and published the anthology with no poems or
photographs removed, raising the necessary £300 from ourselves, our
neighbours and our friends. When, after publication, we sent a
complimentary copy to the Headmaster with our compliments and
best wishes (as we had done to the children's parents and every
local councillor and headmaster in the area) I was sacked from the
school three days later for 'flagrant disobedience', or in the words of
the local authority Divisional Officer 'failure to comply with an
order of a superior officer'. I was offered no hearing or chance to

put my case. This basic right of justice was easily waived by a headmaster who had written books on educational law, and a vice-chairman who as well as being a local vicar, was also an ex-colonial High Court judge.

When the children of the school heard of my dismissal, they organised and launched their own strike. In coming out for me the children were really coming our for themselves. It was *their* poetry and *their* lives that was the issue, and not my disobedience. When the Governors judged the 'Stepney Words' anthology too 'drab', too 'gloomy' and too 'imbalanced' a selection to either sponsor themselves or presume to allow to be published privately, they were demonstrating how much they were threatened by the reality of the children's minds and consciousnesses. They must have 'control' they said. They wanted the 'light' side of local life, they wanted the cockney sparrow to chirp and sing cheerfully from his cage: they didn't want truth and earnestness; they didn't want to hear real people. They didn't want to hear the working class speaking to and consolidating with itself. They wanted all things bright and beautiful at the expense of everything — particularly the truth. A working class child's notion of truth would hardly be a very valid concept to a Chairman of Governors who announces at a Staff/Governors meeting that: "We have to remember that they are all fallen children, that they are all in a state of sin"; or to a headmaster who says that democracy is irrelevant to anyone still at school. Of course 'Stepney Words' is a challenge to people such as these, representing, as they do, the oppressive culture. It had enough truth and insight to question their whole existences as controllers of education:

> No-one wants to wait, listen and
>   look at themselves or what they
>   are doing to what is around them.
> At last they become old and slow
>   and are left behind by the
>   new generation
> Like a new bulb from an old powerhouse.

Intiaz, 14.

As a teacher, I had to examine the two angles. Who was right? The Governors, to arbitrarily prohibit publication and ask me to 'restructure' the anthology excluding both photographs and poems thought too 'drab'? Or the Stepney children, with their honesty and beauty expressed so uncompromisingly? I don't know the Governors, although I know the Vice-Chairman is a local rector, who invites Enoch Powell to speak from his pulpit and follows this sermon up the following week by a sequel given by the local Commissioner of Police. The Headmaster tells me that the governors are all 'good people', and the Chairman, himself a priest, admitted to their hours of 'soul searching' before my dismissal was unanimously confirmed. I know the children and their words. I know something of the level of their truth. I am at school to share my experience with theirs, to work together to discover and change the world. I am not there to a act either as petty censor or evangelist for the tory politics and middle-class life style of the Governors. So we published the poems. A group of people from the community gave, worked and encouraged: teachers, students, a committed photographer, a librarian, a wandering American, a plumber, an Australian, a housewife, a bishop, a clerk, a retired docker and a poet. They all believed in 'Stepney Words'. They all believe, like the children, in the future:

Weeks of preparation for our
Writing to be in print.
Our big chance came for
Something that we could call our own.
And finally the book was published
    and sold.
Everybody liked it, it had the truth
    in it.
But the governors did not like it.

Michele and Cheryl.

On the evening of the first day of the strike at the Sir John Cass and Redcoat School, Stepney (28th May, 1971), Eamonn Andrews asked one of the striking pupils on the 'Today' programme why they had gone on strike, rather than taken some less extreme action. The girl's answer was simple: 'What else could we do?' Within that answer there is the message of frustration and knowledge, despair and desperation, that so many working class children have to tell in the schools, and so many other people tell in their streets, homes and places of work: knowledge of one's own needs and frustration at their lack of fulfilment, despair at the strength of the outside repression, and desperation to break out from it.

'Stepney Words' was only ever seen as something very limited, as a first step into the future. It was a statement of needs; of working class children being able to say for themselves through their poetry, 'This is what we have got, and this is what we lack. Now this is what we need.' This will always be seen as a dangerous direction by the exponents of a system that is more interested in perpetuating its own ends than serving the needs of working class people. 'Stepney Words' gave these children individual and collective respect and attention, and a chance for them to give expression to their own ideas and their own solidarity:

I have my own identity
I have my own ideas
With what should be done to this world.

Tony, 13.

The Education System gives very little consideration and respect to the ideas and identities of children in the East End, just as the social system tends to give very little respect to their parents or those in an any other working class area. Mostly the 'educators' come from outside the area, and commute to evangelise the children and spread their own ideas. Education becomes based on the existences and needs of the educators and their superiors, the upholders of the oppressive culture, and not those of the working class children and their parents. The white middle class consciousness is all: the world of the 'Governors' and the social machine which they administer and serve and finally represent is seen to be the only one to adopt and emulate. They make the decisions, the syllabus, the educational directions and chances for the children. It suits them that in places like the East End the schools should still provide an efficient, semi-literate labour force that makes few demands to share government. There is no training in government at Sir John Cass and Redcoat School, no School Council, no Staff Council or Parent-Teacher Association. The School Governors are priests, middle class church appointees and mostly people living outside of the East End. The Headmaster lives in a spacious Essex suburb. When the parents outside the school asked to see the Headmaster on the second day of the strike, they were threatened with the Law of Trespass.

With the tradition of 'Government' always being distant and out of the reach of most people in the East End, always being an exploitative oppressive force rather than an opportunity for participation, there is a basic hostility to Authority in most people living there. 'Authority' has always meant taking orders from other, 'higher' people — the 'Governors', never something which one has oneself and shares with others. The 'governors' have for generations been those who control, manage and manipulate on every level of life: bosses, landlords, priests, educators. The children and their parents know quite clearly where the political power lies, without having to analyse it theoretically. They know that they have not been given it. The children know particularly because they are right on the end of it. Not even gestures are made to them. They know they are given no rights at all. As Intiaz wrote:

THEM

They don't want truth
They don't want a truthful person
They must have it their way
They are the authorities
We're nothing, just students
We must do as they say
They make the rules
We are forced to obey

And what about the life after school? Children see very clearly what it often offers them. What has a child in a low stream or a middle stream of a secondary school got to lose if he goes on strike against

Ramona, Pauline and *Stepney Words*.

Headmaster and Vice-Chairman of Governors.

his 'governors' for something in which he believes? A CSE or two perhaps? Some patronising words by an overworked housemaster who can find nothing real to say about him on his leaving certificate? Whether he works at school and does his bit of homework or not, there is still the Labour Exchange, the Social Security or working for the 'governors'.

The song which the children were singing outside the school when they were on strike.* (and it was real singing, football crowd singing) was a song which they, and their parents and grandparents and great-grandparents had often sung to each other and to themselves:

> We hate the governors
> Oh yes we do,
> We hate the governors
> Oh yes we do . . .

and singing it together gave a joy, a belief and a recognition of themselves as people with strength and oneness who were prepared to take their rights:

> These were no longer children
> These were people, sticking up for their rights
> The school was painted
> Wall to wall . . .

Michele and Cheryl.

And it was something which was not only child-inspired. There were teachers, parents, school workers involved:

* The children stood in the pouring rain in the playground in protest and refused to go into school. When some of them tried to shelter in the church opposite the Vicar threatened to call the police. "I'm not having you run amok in here!" said the Vicar, who happens to be one of the governors. *Sunday Times.* 12/2/72.

173

Children planned, mothers planned.
Till finally a decision was made.
'Let's strike until he comes back.
Let's sing, let's chant and screem.'
Everybody was with us,
Even the cleaners refused to scrub his
     name from the walls.

Michele and Cheryl.

The children made up poems which they wrote on banners. Jimmy, the 'R form' artist designed a pictorial placard which the children waved while they demonstrated.

Sitting inside a confused and divided staff room, I knew nothing of this at the time of the events. I could only sense a kind of excitement and joy that was never a part of the normal school life. The huge sounds that came from football terraces were now coming from a belief and participation in a cause to which they belonged. The children, with parents behind them, were singing 'We shall not be Moved', 'Roll out the Barrell' (the headmaster's name is Geoffrey Barrell) 'Give Sir a Chance' and 'We Hate the Governors'. I had never heard East End children sing 'We shall Overcome' before, but I was hearing it now. And I didn't know then that the children had chased off to the local newspaper offices the day before to tell them about the impending strike, and that the paper had offered them £50 for the scoop and they had refused, and told the journalists that they were doing this because they believed in it, not because they wanted any money out of it.

It was Thursday morning
All teachers stood helpless . . .

Michele and Cheryl.

The children took the day, as they took the next, as they could take any day that they chose, at any school, anywhere. They were giving a message: 'Remember us. We are strong. Do not play with our lives, because we can beat you. We are massive.' They told the

175

headmaster and governors and teachers that they too had a voice and a force, the force of an organised working class. They told it to the country, so that every teacher whether shouting at his pupils in class or assembly, giving them either respect or insults, sympathy or mystification, now knows something more about working class children and their power and self-respect than he knew before.

And the school broke down. It couldn't function, even though it was, as usual, trying to carry on as if nothing was wrong. When the Deputy Head came out with the class registers with only a handful of the children at school saying, 'Normal Timetable: please go to your classes, the children are waiting', it was like a caricature: Carry on England — will you always carry on, will you never realise?

IS SCHOOL WORTH IT?

What have we learnt at the end of a day at school?
Precisely NOTHING, although facts have been pushed into our minds.
Listening, writing and reading, school consists of.
We're like machines being programmed with orders, we

carry them out, and then we are fed more, It is like
a long string which cannot be digested enough to please
THEM.
I would like to chop the string to leave a loose end
for someone to join up again to a new worthwhile life
at school.

Cheryl, 14.

The string must be chopped, not by 'de-schooling' society, but
by democratising society, and necessarily democratising the schools
as a fundamental part of society. The word 'co-operative' is often
used in the schools. If you are a co-operative pupil, you are normally
quiet, well-behaved and unrebellious. Co-operation is normally seen
in terms of complying obediently with authority, doing what one is
told, recognising and respecting the hierarchy of the school. This idea
of co-operation is, of course, a lie. There can be no mutual respect
amongst people unless co-operation is seen as a fundamental of
democracy, and respect is seen as an actional concept, as people
participating in the decisions and government of their own life-
situation. This must be true in the schools, as it must be in any other
area of life. If it is only true in the schools, then it is still a lie. If
democracy were to exist only in the schools, then education would
continue to be a mystification that the world outside would soon
break, when the school leaver walked into his first job or dole queue.
The only true educational values are democratic values, but that is
only because the only true social and political values are democratic
values. Respect that is not based on equal participation in the
forming of policies and making of decisions, is only a pretence. If
we are all neighbours, we all have ideas and we all have voices:

> True democracy means the real involvement of all the
> members of a community in all the decisions that
> affect that community. And by real involvement we
> do not simply mean the right to vote, but the right to
> participate in an informed way during all stages of
> discussion and to have the absolute certainty that
> once a decision is made it will be carried out promptly
> and efficiently by those entrusted by the community

with this responsibility.*

The hierarchy of the schools only reflects in miniature the hierarchy that has been established at all stages in our society. But it is a hierarchy which is there to show the child what to expect in society in general. The absurd autocracy of the Headmaster in British schools, with his complete control and 'ultimate legal responsibility' for all matters concerning 'the internal organisation, management and discipline of the school', is only a reflection of management in general in the mainstream of British society. The child is made to be conditioned as soon as he arrives in school that there must always be a boss, with a special office or a special dais, standing on the stage every morning in assembly. And the boss must be in charge, that is the first thing he must accept, as must the rank and file of classroom teachers. In this situation the democratic atmosphere can never be allowed to develop and become real. Boredom replaces participation, aggression supplants generosity, and cynicism drives out hope. We need to bring back hope more than anything in the schools. Instead of ticking over, carrying on, only perpetuating themselves, the schools need a vision, and that vision can only be a democratic one. The liberal gestures of one member of staff or one parent on governing bodies, are only tokens. Until the people, the neighbours, who actually use the school also control it, and outside exploiting interest is removed, the schools can never teach the democratic values of generosity and participation. Only by uniting in our pressure and demands as workers and neighbours — parents, teachers, children, — through our trade unions, school councils, staff councils, parent-teacher associations, neighbourhood groups, community presses — for rank and file control of the schools, and all other institutions, to put ourselves in the position of throwing out the enemy culture, and making socialism together, can we move towards a true democratic value system which is the only true Educational standard.

And then, when we have broken all the divisions and walls between us, and we act together as a unified group to take control of our own lives, then, this new season, Charlie, we'll bring Love into the schools. For if we really love our children and want to give

* *Democracy in Schools:* A Rank and File Discussion pamphlet. p.3.

them a society of equity and self-respect which they will grow to control themselves, the real direction of our energy is to struggle towards the structured and organised love of Socialism.

APPENDIX *

A FRIEND IN NEED

Once upon a time a probationary English teacher was teaching a class in a school, when in walked the divisional schools' inspector. As every young teacher knows, all probationary teachers must be inspected by their local education authorities before their probationary years can be passed. The grey-suited, grey-haired man came into the class and announced that he was the Divisional Inspector come to inspect both the teacher's classes and his pupils' exercise books. The twelve-year old pupils were saying, 'Who's he?' and 'What's his game?' as he sat down at a desk near the back of the class. He told them that he was from the I.L.E.A.**, and they said, 'Uhh? What's that?' and 'What's this illy?'

He sat through the class, apparently looking at exercise books of fourth-formers, and taking down notes in a little green book. He seemed very absorbed. At the end of the lesson after the children had gone, he came up to the teacher and began a conversation. He opened his little green book and pointed to some notes which he had made. He had found the word 'bloody' in one of the exercise books, he said, not to mention the word 'arse' which he mentioned next, and the quite unnecessary phrase, 'thinking what you're going to do with your girlfriend at night.' He had taken all three things out of their separate contexts, and had written them down one after another in his little green book. He had taken the word 'bloody' from this poem written by a fifteen-year old boy:

* Most of this appendix was first published in *Rank and File* 16: The Journal of Socialist Teachers.

** Abbreviation for INNER LONDON EDUCATION AUTHORITY.

SOLDIER

I was a soldier
A cockney soldier
A man that was born to die
Only cockney blokes get killed
Stuffy officers stay back safely.

I was a soldier
A cockney soldier
Before I died on the hill
With a bullet through my heart
I clawed my way to Hell.

My brother was a soldier
A bloody good soldier
But he was also born to die.
But he died by being shot
Climbing over the wire back to our trenches.
We both met in Hell.

He said nothing about the poem; what it meant in educational, poetical or political terms or even whether he thought it was good or bad. He only pointed to the word 'bloody' which he had written down in his little green book and said, 'Do you encourage your pupils to use words like that?'

He then went on to point to the phrase to which he had taken an objection. It came from a paragraph which a fifteen-year old boy school-leaver had written on the subject 'Happiness'. This was the whole passage:

Happiness can come in different forms, it could be when you're looking forward to something or you're thinking about what you're going to do to your girl-friend at night. Love can make you happy so I'm told. There is so many things that can make you happy. It is impossible to list. Being happy is an emotion inside you, a built-in personality. People will always like someone

whose happy because it makes them happy too when
they are down in the dumps.

He was fascinated with the phrase which he had picked out; and
asked the teacher whether he thought it was good for children to
write about things like that. When the teacher suggested that perhaps
the inspector thought about them too, and perhaps they also made
him feel happy, he only quickly moved on to his next point in the
little green book. He had noticed the word 'arse' several times in one
poem written by a fourth form girl. 'Do you approve of this?' he
said to the teacher. The teacher looked at the girl's book. She had
written these words in it:

THE RIVER ARSE

The rain is teeming
across the river
falling on the arse of
   a nude girl swimming
without even a splash
   and O it's such a pretty little arse . . .

The inspector had assumed it was the girl's poem. His only comment
was one of disapproval of the use of the word 'arse'. He was a
divisional inspector, a man paid a large salary to inspect young
teachers and pass or fail them for further teaching. He did not know
that this poem was by Brian Patten, a very highly regarded
contemporary poet. He did not recognise that the girl had copied
the poem from 'The Mersey Sound', of which the school had a set,
a poetry anthology which had been a best seller with a huge
influence. No, he had not read the book, he said, and had thought
that the poem had been written by the child. He then read out a list
of some of the subjects — noted in his little green book — on which
the children had written: the local environment, race, dreams, drug
problems, abortion. 'Do you encourage your children to write about
unpleasant things like these?' he said. He then pointed to a poem
written by a fifteen-year old boy, called 'The Washing', and through
some very strange and personal psychedelic vision of his own

suggested it was about 'drugs':

> I have just seen my mother's washing,
> They still look dirty though,
> But my mother's nosing
> Looking at the dirty washing
> Hoping it might fade away.
>
> She washed a white shirt,
> She tried to make it clean,
> But when she hung it on the line,
> It was the ugliest sight you have seen.

The teacher had some difficulty in understanding these things: an inspector posing as an authority on the teaching of English unaware of the most popular and widely-read book of English poetry for years, a man responsibly placed in the educational hierarchy with an interest in English, unable to admit the fine qualities of a child's poem and only seeking to cut it to pieces and destroy it, a man disinterested in a child's notion of happiness, a man set up as the custodian of children's imaginations who will only rip apart their expression for his own prurient motives, and make his own vicious and absurd interpretations.

But the teacher was learning fast.

The inspector clapped his little green book shut, and as he left the classroom, beneath what looked like a smile he turned to the teacher and said, 'Remember that the divisional inspector is the teacher's friend, not his enemy.' He went out through the door and straight down to the Headmaster's office and stayed with him for over an hour. They both lived happily ever after.

IN THE CHURCH OF THE

Parish of St. Botolph-without-Aldgate

Rector: REV. DEREK HARBORD, One of Her Majesty's Judges (rtd.)

and of the

Ward of Portsoken

Alderman: SIR BERNARD WALEY-COHEN, Bt., Lord Mayor 1960-61

Commemoration of Sir John Cass, Kt.

sometime Alderman of this Ward whose munificence founded and endowed

Sir John Cass's Foundation School

The congregation being seated, the styles and titles of the Founder shall be declared by the Chairman of the Foundation:

> Give thanks to God for SIR JOHN CASS, Knight. Born and baptised in this parish of St. Botolph and Ward of Portsoken, he founded our School in 1710.
>
> He was sometime Master of the Worshipful Company of Carpenters, Master of the Worshipful Company of Skinners, Alderman of this Ward of Portsoken. Sheriff of London and a member of Parliament for the City.
>
> Born February 20th 1661, he died in his 58th year on the 5th day of July, 1718 in the act of signing the Will by which his school is still endowed.
>
> Give thanks to God for SIR JOHN CASS.

Response: Thanks be to God.

All shall stand, and while the school hymn is being sung, the Chairman and the Clerk, preceded by the Mace, shall move to the Northex and there place a wreath of laurel before the monument of the Founder.

Then, all kneeling, these prayers shall be offered:

> I live in a very large house. There are very few houses down the street because they are taken over by large flats and maceanets. Opposite me there are a block of Jewish flats and the people in there are always fighting and rowing. I don't mind the area all that much but I would like to move a little way away, my Mum does not like it, and she would like to move to the country but my Dad and us do not want to. We are surrouned by a cematry, a old mans home and a mental hospital. Some times the people from the mental hospital go down to Mile End station and jump under the trains. The other night I was coming home from a club and I saw one of the pations out of the hospital houlding up all the lorries going by. There are quite some good clubs like the A-train and a few others. My Dad would never move into flats, becuase he likes to do things in the garden and things around the house,

185

which you can not do in flates. Now all the houses have been pulled down round our area all exspert our street, which will be coming down in a copy of years time. I would like to move to Kent where my sister and her husband lives.

Let us pray for the school:

BLESS, O Lord, the school, and use it to further the coming of thy kingdom. May thy presence ever be within its walls, and may it stand always for what is good. Grant that the children and teachers may so gain from its life that many shall bless thee for the day when it was founded, and may its work be continued and prospered for the the generations to come;
through Jesus Christ our Lord, AMEN.

Just off of Commercial Road is a long shaby market called Watney Street. Off of Watney Street is the road where I live. Chapman Street is a long, straight road, which is very narrow. It's a depressing road, made of cobble stones with paches of tar where the road has broken. There a little pub on the corner and my building is the first block from it. On one side of the road is a railway station Shadwell and on the other side is my estate. Built in under the arches are garages and what make the more depressing is in one of the arches is a colour man names Jimmy make wooden coffins, and all you can here is the saw cutting the wood. This saw as well as the train cut the picture out or make it roll. The street is always empty of people a part from the locel gang from Cannon Street are around.

Let us pray for the Headmaster and staff:

O HEAVENLY Father, we pray for the Headmaster and Staff of the School. May thy HOLY SPIRIT inspire them at all times in the discharge of their duties. Fill their hearts with loyalty, courage and patience, so that in all things they may seek thy glory and the well-being of the school.
through Jesus Christ our Lord, AMEN.

I live in old flats with a fire escape
which they use for a washing line
the old rusted fire escape makes the buldings look
even older.
I wish i could make into a brand new home
with a drive way that never ends
and doors were as big as the house itself with a door knocker
that no one would touch because they thought it was two
valuable.
the house would have two swimming pools of course olympic
size. the grass would rise in the spring and the
bees would buzz around rose and take the honey to their
babes. I would stand and watch them and let nature take its
place, but as spring comes to its end and winter begins to
draw the spider builds his cobweb house to live there till the
spring.

Let us pray for the Governors and Managers.

*ALMIGHTY God, bless with thy wisdom and inspire with thy
love the Governors of the Foundation and the managers of the
school. Grant that they may direct all things according to thy will,
and use the gifts of bounty bestowed upon the School to thy honour
and glory, and to the good of thy children;
through Jesus Christ our Lord. AMEN.*

I live in a flat. I have lived in a house with to big gardens.
One at the back of the house and one at the front. It was free
floars high. My nan lived downstairs. We had the top and the
midle of the house. We could have eney animal we wanted, In
there and mack as much noise as we wanted to. We lived there
right until I was twelve. but now we are living in a flat. It has
now garden just a little balcony. We can only have fish or a
cage bird. We can't have eney dog's, cat's or toetoises like we
used to In our old house. I think it was much better in our old
house. than living in a flat. You didnt yous to have every body
frowing there rubish on the Steps. And we had our own
dustbin we didn't have every one els droping there rubish

as they frow it away like they do now when they put it In the
shoot. Some time they will empty there bins about half past
eleven at night just as I am falling asleep. The circar it o.k.
where I live now there is now were where your child could run
you only have a little park down the back but you couldn't
let your child down there if it was only about 2 year old they
they start geting there hands In every thing.

While all remain standing, the Rector shall pronounce the blessing.
Then to be sung, as the procession leaves the Chancel.

SIR JOHN CASS

John Oxlade, 1946

Let us thank the Christ for all who did
    their duty.
Famous men of old and great of heart in
    fight;
Who fought their way and laboured for
    their day,
        And strove to make our England
        A happy, lovely England,
Happy in his praise and lovely in his light.

Now they thank the Christ who called them
    to be captains;
Now they sing his praise in everlasting light;
And still they pray, they pray the Lord
    today
        That he would make our England
        A happy, lovely England,
Happy in his praise and lovely in his light.

Let us pray the Christ that he would make
    us soldiers
Truer in his ways and braver in his fight;
That we, as they, may loyally obey,

And help to make our England
A happy, lovely England,
Happy in his praise and lovely in his light.

J.M.C. Crum.

Sir John Cass, a City merchant and Alderman, died in 1718. In the moment of his death he signed away a portion of his riches to found a school for East End children. He died coughing up blood, which made the white quill he was using turn red. Now, every year on 'Founder's Day' the children of the school are marched to Aldgate Church, where they hear a service of remembrance to his beneficence, and are given red feathers for their buttonholes.

THE DEATH OF SIR JOHN CASS

Sir John Cass lay at death's dark door,
His time was nearly come.
'Oh how can I requite my life
And the bad deeds I have done?'

He coughed and groaned like living death
And grimly clenched his teeth.
'Oh how can I stave off this hell
And the Devil's land beneath?'

He took his quill, so soft and white,
And scraped upon the page.
'Oh God in Heaven, pure and bright,
Give mercy in my age.'

'I have been christian, good and rich
All through my merchant life,
Why do I see this endless ditch
Of fire and hate and strife?'

'I hereby leave my money here
But I must go above —
If gold has made my life on earth,
At least I'll die with love.'

'My money goes to found a school
For cheerful East End folk,
And they will love me one and all
And go to church by rote.'

As John Cass died he spluttered blood
And made his quill dark red.
His hand dropped down, and made a thud
And the will fell from his bed.

His words were kept, a school was built,
And Stepney's children entered,
And through the gold of rich men's guilt
Their hearts and minds were splintered.

And Governors spoke through harnessed hearts,
'Be grateful for this school.
We gave it, do not talk of rights
It's us who make the rules.'

'Get your heads down to the desks,
Remember they are ours,
Obey, and take no upstart risks
Or damnation will be yours,

'We have the power, the money, the right,
Do not presume too much.
We'll live to run your lives for you,
You'll always need our crutch.'

John Cass still smiles in Aldgate Church,
His ghost haunts Stepney Way,
Along Commercial Road it lurks
Still counting out its pay.

But now you young all through this land
Don't do your master's duty,
Take the new world by the hand
And carve your own fresh beauty.